Letting Them Go

Letting Them Go

Dave Veerman

INTEGRITY®
PUBLISHERS

family

Nashville

LETTING THEM GO

Published by Integrity Publishers, a division of Integrity Media, Inc., 5250 Virginia Way, Suite 110, Brentwood, TN 37027.

HELPING PEOPLE WORLDWIDE EXPERIENCE *the* MANIFEST PRESENCE OF GOD.

Cover design: Brand Navigation, www.brandnavigation.com
Interior design: Teresa Billingsley

Library of Congress Cataloging-in-Publication Data
Veerman, David.
Letting them go / Dave Veerman.
p. cm.
Summary: "Helping parents get ready for the day their child leaves home"—Provided by publisher.
Tradepaper
ISBN-13: 978-1-5914-5388-8
ISBN-10: 1-59145-388-7

1. Parenting—Religious aspects—Christianity. 2. Christian teenagers
—Religious life. 3. Parent and teenager—Religious aspects—Christianity.
1. Title.
BV4529.V43 2006
248.845—dc22
2005031641

06 07 VG 9 8 7 6 5 4 3 2 1

DEDICATION

For Kara and Dana
miracle babies
terrific kids
amazing adults
Mom and Dad are so proud of you!

ACKNOWLEDGMENTS

Thanks to special friends Bruce and Mitzie Barton,
Ruth Haley Barton, Brian Bobbitt, Jim Burns,
Ron DiCianni, Madeleine Garber, Claudia Gerwin,
David and Gwen Hubbard, Jerry Jenkins, Larry Kreider,
Chuck Lewis, Dottye Luttrell, Laura Minchew, John Ortberg,
Gary Rosberg, Betsy Schmitt, Mary Manz Simon, Babs Swanson,
Linda Taylor, Becky Tirabassi, and Neil Wilson
for their valuable counsel and contributions to this work.

TABLE OF CONTENTS

INTRODUCTION

It's nearly time, the moment you have anticipated for almost eighteen years. At first the goal seemed so distant that you hardly thought of it at all. Like setting out on a long trip when you know your destination and you have a pretty good idea how to get there, each day's concerns and mileage grab your attention. And before you know it, you've arrived. During the past few years, as the months rolled by at an ever-quickening pace, you occasionally felt a twinge and recalled those younger, more innocent days. "Where has the time gone?" you whisper.

Just the other day, it seems, you returned from the hospital with your freshly bundled, newest member of the family. Then you tried to keep up with your growing toddler and chauffeured him or her to all the lessons, clubs, and events. During the whirl-wind tween and teen years, you plotted classes and homework together and talked about the future. Now, suddenly, you're standing at the threshold of "letting go" and releasing your child to the world—still an adolescent but nearly an autonomous adult.

Regardless of your trepidations, it's not all bad, you know. In fact, check out this list:

The Top Ten Advantages of Your Child's Leaving Home

10. You will significantly reduce your number of bank accounts and investments (less money to have to worry about).
9. You will finally see the floor of your teenager's room.
8. You will get to redeem all of your airline frequent-flyer miles.
7. You will be able to use the bathroom much sooner.
6. You will regain control over the family's cars.
5. You will learn how to wire money.
4. You won't have to arise at 5:30 a.m. to go sit in the wind and rain for three-hour soccer games.

3. Your throat will heal (sore and hoarse from all the cheering).

2. During vacation breaks, you will experience life with someone who now knows just about everything.

1. You will have something to talk about with other parents in the same situation.

There—do you feel better?

A Significant Passage

Whether it's going to college, joining the military, or entering the work force, leaving home is a significant passage both for kids and their parents. For young people, leaving home means becoming an adult—being out in the world with the freedom to make decisions, released from childhood restraints. They can find this exciting, exhilarating, and a little scary. For parents, this can also be a time of celebration and joy. Some, however, dread this day, struggle when it happens, and grieve long afterward.

We parents knew this day would come, of course. Actually,

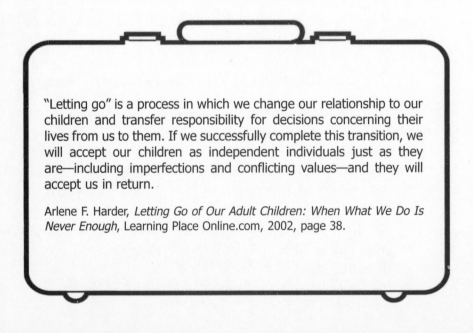

"Letting go" is a process in which we change our relationship to our children and transfer responsibility for decisions concerning their lives from us to them. If we successfully complete this transition, we will accept our children as independent individuals just as they are—including imperfections and conflicting values—and they will accept us in return.

Arlene F. Harder, *Letting Go of Our Adult Children: When What We Do Is Never Enough*, Learning Place Online.com, 2002, page 38.

we planned and prepared for it, or so we thought. It's not the end of life as we know it, you know. Good parents want their children to grow up and leave home. When that happens, it usually means that we've done something right! We certainly wouldn't want the kids to live with us for another decade or beyond. But knowing all that, we still can feel unprepared. The day came too quickly.

Ken Davis explains:

> I remember vividly the day Traci was born. It could have been yesterday. I looked and fell instantly in love with a little package of life. She was the most beautiful thing in the world. The doctor asked if I would like to hold her. "No," I said. If I touched her, I knew she would break. But the doctor assured me she could survive the ordeal and laid her in my arms.
>
> How light she was! How beautiful she appeared through the soft blur of my tears! Then I made a terrible mistake. I blinked. In an instant eighteen years went by.
>
> When I opened my eyes she was still in my arms, tears still in my eyes. But she was no longer a baby. She was a beautiful young woman and I was saying good-bye. Leaving Traci in a small college dorm room was one of the hardest things I have done in my life. (from *The Punch Line*, Ken Davis newsletter, Volume 9, Number 1–November, 1993, page 2)

This parent and thousands of others each year identify much more with the expressions of this list:

The Top Ten Disadvantages of Your Child's Leaving Home

10. You've lost your expert adolescent arguer.
9. You have to feed the dog, shovel the walk, and cut the grass (those were your kid's jobs—oh wait; you're doing them already).
8. You learn what "home equity" means.

7. You learn that no cell phone plans come with enough minutes.

6. You daydream about your student's classes, dates, spiritual life, etc.

5. Your next-oldest child now thinks that he or she is "king of the hill."

4. You set one less place at the table.

3. You've lost your "gofer."

2. You no longer learn all that great stuff that you picked up while helping with homework.

1. Your house is much too quiet.

A Big Surprise

The Boy Scouts' familiar motto states, "Be Prepared." That's a great idea but often difficult to pull off. Many times, after an

And so it has come down to this: You're going, really going. Oh, you'll be back. It isn't as if I will never see you again. But when you return, you'll come as a guest. For all practical purposes, you are gone for good.

Though you'll always remain in my heart and be a member of our family, nothing will be the same. While I may finance your life-style temporarily, you are now your own person, making your own decisions, disciplining or not disciplining yourself.

It's stunning to realize that the clichés are true. All those platitudes I heard last week, when you were born, are now indisputable. "Hang on to every moment, every day," I was told when I showed you off as our new arrival. "Before you know it, they'll be gone."

Jerry Jenkins, *As You Leave Home* (Colorado Springs, CO: Focus on the Family Publishing, 1993), 3–4.

event, where hindsight is 20/20, we remark with regret, "I should have _____," and we fill in the blank with what would have been adequate preparation.

I didn't know how I would react when my older daughter, Kara, left for college. I had heard stories, of course, from relatives, neighbors, and friends. So I knew about this time of transition and thought I would be ready. But I have to admit that my feelings caught me by surprise.

The unsettling truth is that life often blindsides us. Yes, we can prepare for rain by noting the weather forecast, wearing a raincoat, and carrying an umbrella. We can prepare for tough economic times by stashing funds in a bank or the stock market "for a rainy day." We can even prepare for the birth of a new family member by decorating the baby's room, stocking shelves with Pampers and Gerbers, and practicing the dash to the hospital. But so much of life is unpredictable. We can't turn to the "Child Channel" and learn that today we should expect "showers of rebellion" or an afternoon of "partly sunny disposition," or hear the warning of "watch for flu-like symptoms next week."

Even so, there is a huge difference between being somewhat prepared and being caught totally off guard. We may not know what lies down the trail through the woods at night, but we'll do better if we have a flashlight and fresh batteries as we begin our journey.

That pretty much describes parenting, doesn't it? We get a trail and a flashlight, but often we're still pretty much in the dark with no idea of what lies around each turn in the path. In fact, the longer we parent, the less confident we become. Rearing children is complicated, and we don't have as many answers as we once thought.

It's great that we have a God who knows us thoroughly (Psalm 139:1–18), cares for us deeply (Matthew 6:25–34), and stands by us always (Matthew 28:20; John 14:16). Our loving Father knows the path ahead and has promised his strength, comfort, guidance, and peace (check out Romans 8:26–39) to us and to our children.

This book was written to help you prepare, highlighting God's truths and sharing practical advice. I can't promise that you'll find everything you should know and everything you should do to prepare for every aspect of this parenting passage, but these chapters can shed a bit more light on the subject, explaining what you can expect around the bend. And it helps to know that others have traveled the same path and to learn from their experiences.

So how do you prepare for this new phase in your life and in the life of your child? And how can you let go with no regrets? Those are important questions this book will answer. Watching a son or daughter emerge from the chrysalis and fly off as a fully formed butterfly should be an exhilarating and joyful experience. We need to prepare our minds for the change. We need to prepare our hearts.

The problem with
being a parent is that
by the time
you're experienced,
you're out of work.
—Wayne Rice

Chapter 1

AM I MISSING SOMETHING?
(LIKE THE LAST EIGHTEEN YEARS!)

Watch out! Be careful! Don't forget! Make sure you . . .

Life is filled with warnings. We've been on the receiving end of plenty of them—highway signs ("Bridge out"), prescription bottles ("May cause drowsiness"), fences ("Beware of dog"), appliances ("Do not immerse"), SUVs ("Higher rollover risk"), and TV ads ("Do not try this at home!"), to name a few. And as parents, we've certainly issued a multitude of warnings to our kids:

- Keep doing that and your eyes will stay that way!

- Don't eat so fast, or you'll choke!

- Wear your coat so you don't catch a cold.

- Some day you'll have kids of your own, and we'll see how you like it!

Giving warnings seems to come with the territory—it's part of being a good parent.

Well, now we're back at the receiving end. And I offer a few warnings as you approach this momentous event, this turning point in your parenting experience. Some of these may sound familiar, but that's okay; just "proceed with caution!"

Looking Back

Warning #1: This time of letting go will feel familiar.

Remember when your child was born? Just yesterday, it seems. And remember when you put your excited and nervous "baby" on the school bus for the first time? Now that was a traumatic "letting go" event.

Even if they don't put their children on a bus, most parents feel insecurity, fear, and sadness when they send them off to

For four lightening-fast years she'd been ours and ours alone. And now that was all going to change.

We'd put her to bed last night as "our girl"—exclusive property of Mommy and Daddy. Mommy and Daddy read to her, taught her, listened to her. But beginning today, someone else would, too.

Until today, it was Mommy and Daddy who wiped away the tears and put on the Band-Aids. But beginning today, someone else would, too.

I didn't want to wake her.

Until today, her life was essentially us—Mom, Dad, and baby sister Andrea. Today that life would grow—new friends, a teacher. Her world was this house—her room, her toys, her swing set. Today her world would expand. She would enter the winding halls of education—painting, reading, calculating . . . becoming.

I didn't want to wake her. Not because of the school. It's a fine one. Not because I don't want her to learn. Heaven knows I want her to grow, to read, to mature. Not because she doesn't want to go. School has been all she could talk about for the last week!

No, I didn't want to wake her up because I didn't want to give her up.

Max Lucado, *Six Hours One Friday* (Portland, OR: Multnomah Books, 1989), 47–48).

school. And parents are surprised by their feelings, as what was supposed to be an exciting day begins to fill them with anxiety and dread.

I used to witness this dramatic scene at the end of August every year because I lived next to an elementary school. On the first day of classes, parents would parade past my home with their little ones. Dressed up for the important occasion, most of the children seemed excited about the prospects. A few, however, would cry, not wanting to leave Mommy or Daddy. Many of the parents wielded video cameras, recording the momentous occasion, and all of them seemed a little saddened as they said their good-byes to their children and then turned and walked away.

Was that your experience? Babs Swanson remembers:

> Kindergarten was difficult because it felt I was no longer able to carefully choose Brooke's environment. It felt as if Dave and I were thrusting her out into the cold, cruel world.
>
> I wanted to send her off each day "right." I remember one winter day when I knelt down in front of her, all bundled up, and told her that I love her, Jesus loves her and is with her, how precious she is . . . and she interrupted me saying: "Mom, your teeth are yellow—could be plaque." So much for that special moment!

So, at your first letting-go experience what happened? What did you learn? My guess is that despite the initial sadness, you began to appreciate you and your child's new adventure. And as your son or daughter returned from school each day, you celebrated his or her return and enjoyed hearing tales from the playground and classroom. Sure, you had difficult moments when you had to nurse a physical or emotional wound, but you loved watching your child explore a new world of facts, skills, and relationships and grow

> Parenthood can be difficult, but it also has its rewards. In the end, there's no substitute for the sense of satisfaction that comes from watching as your children, under your steady guiding hand, develop from tiny, helpless Frequent Barfer modules into full-grown, self-reliant young adults fully capable of crashing your car into a day-care center.
>
> Dave Barry

mentally, socially, and emotionally. You didn't even mind helping with homework.

This experience and the first year of school also stretched your faith, as you prayed for your child's safety and trusted him or her to God's care. And I think that if you are honest, upon reflection you would have to say that despite the sadness of the moment, this first experience of letting go wasn't all that bad. God was faithful.

You probably learned a few lessons too, about time and the brevity of life. At no time is this more evident and felt more deeply than when we send our children off into the world, on their own. Just yesterday, it seems, we cradled them gently in the hospital and then brought them home. And who can forget those sleepless but prayerful nights of rocking, singing, and comforting our babies? But the next thing we knew, we were sending them off to school; then suddenly, they were teenagers.

Now we've come to this critical juncture, the moment of truth, when we watch them fly off on their own. And we wonder where the time went.

Experiencing this reality of the brevity of life brings us face-to-face with another biblical challenge. Moses prayed, "Teach us to make the most of our time, so that we may grow in wisdom" (Psalm 90:12). The King James Version rendering uses the phrase "number our days."

Clearly God is challenging us to be good stewards of our time, of the years, months, weeks, days, hours, minutes, and moments that he has entrusted to us. We have a finite number of years left. We must not squander such a valuable commodity.

Regardless of how you dealt with letting go in the past, you're approaching another release point. And those years have gone so quickly, one after the other, increasing in speed (or so it seemed) as our kids got older. But remembering that earlier time of release and how you successfully navigated it should give you hope during this one. You made it before, and it was good; you can make it again.

FACING THE FACTS

Warning #2: Watch out for denial.

You've probably heard the old saying, "Denial ain't just a river in Egypt!" It points out our tendency to ignore the truth when confronted with distasteful realities. Evidently, the "denial river" runs through all of us. We can deny, for example, that we are aging and refuse to act our age. We can ignore physical symptoms until confronted with a serious diagnosis. Alcoholics and other addicts are famous for refusing to acknowledge their "problem." Carried to the extreme, some people live in a fantasy world, divorced almost completely from reality.

We respond to bad news and unsettling circumstances with denial, because we don't like pain or, perhaps, simply because we want life to remain constant, the way we like it. But we need to accept the truth, deal with it, and move on.

> Every one of our kids began to act more grown-up once they got the driver's license. They were more cooperative and more considerate.
>
> Bruce and Mitzie Barton

So listen carefully to this statement (and don't be shocked): some parents can't believe their little child has grown up and is leaving home! And when that happens, it's bad for everyone involved: parents, child, and the rest of the family.

So that's why I say that the first step in letting go is to face the facts, to accept reality. Again, it's helpful to learn from a reality in our past, in this case, not that long ago. Remember when your "baby" was almost sixteen and wanted to take driver's ed? A recording of one of those sessions might sound something like this:

That's good; you put your seat belt on, checked the rearview mirror, made sure the radio, windshield wipers, and turn signals all work, and started the car. But, uh, you might want to close the door before pulling out. You're doing fine now. Just a little faster would be okay. Uh, don't worry about the honking, just push down a little bit more and ease up and beyond fifteen miles per hour. Yes, maybe it would be good to get off the expressway. Get off at the next exit. No! Not here! I meant the next exit—two miles down the road. But you made it. By the way, it's always good to be in the right hand lane when you exit right. You don't think those other drivers minded that you cut them off like that? Uh, Miss Anderson, they weren't waving at

When we dropped Charity off at college as a freshman, I couldn't help but remember her first day of kindergarten. I had walked to school that day to pick her up, and as we made our way home, she insisted on walking a couple blocks ahead. I called her back and tried to convince her to walk and talk with me, but she said, "Can we do that when we get home? I want to be a big girl." There was neither malice nor impertinence. Just the honest expression of a little girl trying to grow up.

So we walked that way, and I had the pleasure of watching her walk ahead of me—ponytail bobbing, backpack carried proudly. Every block or so she would turn around and wave—just making sure I was there. And I would wave back, trying to communicate with every wave that I loved her and was proud of her and that it was okay that she wanted to walk alone. And it has been that way every since, it seems. That simple walk home was a picture of the process parents and children begin at birth, the process of letting go and allowing our children to gain their independence little by little. It is, after all, what we raise them for.

Adapted from Ruth Haley Barton, *The Truths That Free Us* (Colorado Springs, CO: Shaw Publishing, 2002), 169–70.

you; they were . . . never mind. Okay . . . now we're coming to a red light, so slow down. No, take your foot OFF
the gas pedal and put it on the brake pedal . . . NOT SO
HARD! That's all right—I had my shoulder harness in
place and I'll recover in a couple of months from the
whiplash. The light is green so you can go now. I know
that light is red, but your light is green, so pull ahead;
don't mind the honking behind us. Now that was a beautiful right turn—probably one of the best turns I've seen
in a long time. You're welcome. But we're on a one-way
street! Yes, I know you're only going one way, but it's
the wrong way. Do you notice all those cars coming at
us and swerving? Wait—why are you backing up so
fast? You want to go the right way? Whoa! How did
you do that? A quick-180-degree turn? Oh, you saw it
on TV. Hmmm. Well, at least we're going the right
direction. What does a flashing light mean? Well, if
it's a flashing yellow light, it means caution, and a
flashing red means . . . wait a minute, where did you see
one? In the rearview mirror . . . on top of the blue and
white car . . . I see. No, wait, it doesn't mean step on the
gas. I don't care if you did see it on TV.

Ideally, you want your son or daughter to leave at the right time for
the right reasons; the details will vary from family to family and child
to child. But you'll know when it comes. If you're ready and if your
kids are ready, just like childbirth, it will be a time of joy and
celebration for everyone involved as well as a time of some pain and
struggle.

Wayne Rice, *Cleared for Takeoff* (San Diego, CA: UYT Books, 2000), 203.

Driving and driver's training has made great material for comedians for several decades. We laugh because we identify with the student and imagine what the instructor must be feeling, and because we've been at the mercy of less-than-competent drivers. But it's no laughing matter when we picture our teenage son or daughter behind the wheel. That's a different story. And having the child get that driver's license was another occasion of letting go.

A steel and plastic vehicle, worth thousands of dollars, powered by internal explosions, and guided by an inexperienced adolescent hurtling headlong at incredible speeds down rain- and snow-slicked highways in the company of other drivers, many of whom may be incompetent, irresponsible, or under the influence of alcohol or drugs—that's the sobering vision of parents concerned for their potential driver. It's not a pretty picture, and certainly not funny.

Driving means independence and freedom, so getting the license was a rite of passage for our teenagers. This was also a significant milestone for us as parents as we encountered a variety of emotions and conflicts. Of course we knew our insurance premiums would increase dramatically, and we would incur other related expenses. But those didn't bother us nearly as much as the idea of our "little child" actually driving a car. And vivid memories of our own teenage driving experiences made this reality even more difficult to accept. We remembered the risks we took and what we did and where we went in our cars. Some of those events we've never confessed to anyone else, certainly not our kids. No wonder we were hesitant and suspicious.

Even when parents have done everything right and their teenagers have performed in an exemplary manner and have given no reason for doubt, these loving moms and dads still worry. Letting go is tougher when it may be a life-or-death matter. We knew the statistics; we read the news reports; we remembered our first near accident and road trip.

Yet we handed over the keys and watched our child/adult drive off. We faced reality.

So now that you've had a few years of teenage driving behind you, how did it go? What did you learn about yourself, your faith, and your prayer life? Better yet, what did your son or daughter learn?

Hopefully your teenager's lessons included taking responsibility for his or her actions; being faithful to your trust; learning how to navigate in an adult world (and on the highways); and other skills. Your son or daughter probably also learned something about freedom and autonomy.

You also gained a new family chauffeur! And you successfully let go a little bit more.

We can learn much from those past experiences. Although the temptation to deny reality was strong, we faced the facts, released our grip a bit, and guided our child successfully through that passage. And we all survived—probably thrived! So the challenge is to choose that same positive, realistic attitude at this next event.

And that leads to our next consideration.

DEALING WITH EMOTIONS

Warning #3: This will be an emotional experience.

You've heard the jokes that begin, "I have good news and bad news. What do you want to hear first?" Then comes the punch line: "The good news is that your teenage son made it home before curfew. The bad news: he arrived in the back of a squad car."

We chuckle because those jokes mirror life. It's the consistency of most of our experiences—a mixture of good and bad, positive and negative, happy and sad. Even in a purely delightful moment, we feel a twinge of sadness because we know the moment will end. No wonder we long for heaven and unending bliss.

In addition, soon into adulthood we realized how quickly the years pass. When we were young and had all of life ahead of us, we didn't think that much about the future. Sure, we had read, "For your life is like the morning fog—it's here a little while, then it's gone (James 4:14), but we thought we had forever." Even at the birth of that first child, life seemed to move at a snail's pace as we changed diapers, fed, burped, put down for a nap, comforted, and on and on. Suddenly, however, the days, months, and years seemed to blur as they too quickly passed. We begin careers, get married, have children, and, the next thing we know, our kids are about to leave home. From birth to third grade seems to take thirty years, and from third grade to college—three minutes! Recently, you've realized how quickly the years pass.

No wonder "letting go" is huge. As we just mentioned, we had glimpses and smaller doses of this experience earlier:

- Sending them to school for the first time

- Helping them prepare for the first dates

- Watching them drive off, clutching those newly minted drivers' licenses

- Praying for their safety on the mission trips

And here we go again.

The Beginning

The reality of letting go, and the emotional jolt, began for me at the graduation of my elder daughter, Kara. She had enjoyed a great senior year in high school; in fact, all four years had been good—not too tough and filled with activities and accomplishments.

I had heard reports from other parents about tearful graduation ceremonies, but at the time, I couldn't relate. My own high school career hadn't been that difficult; in fact, I surmised, a person would have to try hard *not* to graduate. So why all the emotion? Graduation was a rite of passage, of course, but not that big of a deal—or so I thought.

Then, suddenly, on that bright and windy day in June, Kara walked in line with her classmates, across the platform constructed on the football stadium (with the true fans in the stands), and received her diploma. And I joined the throng of emotional parents of graduations past and fought back my tears. Reality hit like a lightening bolt out of the clear June sky: "those high school days are behind us and soon our 'little girl' will be gone!" Afterward, misty-eyed, I congratulated Kara and hugged her close.

I wasn't surprised entirely by my feelings, but I was surprised by their depth. And while the graduation ceremony surfaced these emotions, they emerged again, with even more intensity, a couple of months later when we sent her off to college. These feelings were mixed: good news and bad; joy and sorrow; celebration and grief.

The Joy

In this emotional stew, certainly joy is in the mix with parties, promises, and plans for the future. The joy is shared with the graduate; parent and child rejoice together.

Milestone

First, we realize that high school graduation is a significant marker. For many kids, high school graduation will be their biggest accomplishment in life. School awards and honors and the gifts and loving expressions of relatives and friends heighten the meaning of this event. Add to this the fact that high school graduation is a highly regarded occasion in American society.

So celebrations ensue—parties, open houses, and presents. And we rejoice with our sons and daughters as they receive the heartfelt congratulations of their grandparents, siblings, cousins, uncles, aunts, neighbors, teachers, coaches, pastors, choir directors, youth leaders, and close friends.

Achieved Goals

We also are joyful because we realize that graduation marks the end of a long process. In junior high, grades were important because your student's academic record would determine the courses he or she could take in high school. In high school, grades were important because they would determine what your student could do or where he or she could go afterward. So at high school graduation ceremonies, parents sort of breathe a collective sigh of relief: We've passed. The pressure's off. We did it! Hooray!

If the graduate has been accepted into a desired college or has made a career decision, then this occasion really does, as graduation speakers emphasize annually, mark the first step forward in the rest of their lives.

Victory

Many families rejoice because high school graduation symbolizes a major victory over a nearly relentless parade of enemies during the past several years.

> • Caren and her parents struggled mightily to balance homework, friends, dates, sports, and church activities.

- Jonathan limps slightly as he walks to accept his diploma. But he's walking, having survived a near-fatal automobile accident.

- Kris battled anorexia nervosa during most of ninth and tenth grade. But she conquered those demons.

- Drugs nearly claimed Michael, but now he's clean.

- Attempting to fit in with his new school, Devon made a series of bad choices, propelling him in the wrong direction. But the prayers of his parents and the intervention of a caring youth pastor turned him around.

- Juan still bears evidence of his battle with cancer. But the disease is in remission, and he passed all his classes.

Life can be hard and adolescence treacherous. So the parents of these graduates have great reason to exult, joyfully and with thanksgiving. Feeling as though they have left those troubles behind, they look forward, optimistically, to the future.

Maturity

We also feel joy because our graduates exhibit a sense of maturity—they certainly look grown-up—and they have survived many normal trials and tribulations to this point, including junior high, puberty, driver's ed, dating, gym classes, auditions, tryouts, and peer pressure. We sense that they are turning out okay; maybe we did some things right after all.

You may have noticed this change for the better during the previous year, when discussing college choices and, then, making campus visits. Or perhaps you have been impressed with your son or daughter's stated career goals and preliminary plans.

At this point, I need to add that some parents of eighteen-year-olds experience the opposite. Their kids have dropped out, spaced out, or freaked out. They continue to struggle with adjusting their dreams and expectations for their kids. While most young people this age are moving out and beyond high school, parents of the other teens have a rough road of prayer ahead. I encourage you to love them unconditionally and nurture your relationship.

Challenges

Joy also comes for young people themselves when they arrive at the college campus, military base, or new job. Excited by the prospects ahead and the fresh experiences, they feel ready for the challenges.

Our kids may harbor a little apprehension about being away from home, in a new situation, but usually their exhilaration will overshadow any anxiety they may be feeling. Or they will mask their fears; after all, now they are independent and on their own.

In considering milestones, achieved goals, victory, maturity, and challenges, perhaps you could identify with several of those reasons for happiness. So take a moment or two right now and count your blessings. Thank God for each one and for the child-near-adult he has blessed you with. Then rejoice. Repeat this step often. When you feel the sadness and burden, pull out this list and pray a prayer of thankfulness.

The Sorrow

Most parents expect to be happy about a son or daughter graduating from high school and moving on with life. What surprises them the most is the sorrow, the almost overwhelming feeling of sadness they experience when they drive away, leaving sons and daughters behind.

Visit a nearby college in the fall, at the end of new student/parent orientation, and you'll observe a steady stream of moms and dads walking slowly toward their cars. With shoulders slumped as though carrying a heavy burden, Dad fights his tears. Mom doesn't hold back, and you'll see her freely wiping her eyes.

I heard a mother explaining that she had cried just about the whole three-hour trip home from the university where she had left her son. Then she exclaimed, "Why do I feel like someone has just died? And what can I do about it?"

That's exactly how I felt when Gail and I left Kara at college.

And guess what—I had the same experience with almost the same emotions four years later when Gail and I repeated the process with Dana. Sure, the feeling wasn't quite as intense because I knew the routine. But I was sad again and needed a few days to get back to normal.

Perhaps the primary cause of our sadness is simply the knowledge that change is in the air. Most of us don't deal well with changes of any kind, especially the ones that seem to rip the fabric of our lives. Big life changes can be extremely difficult to deal with. In fact, psychologists and other counselors call these primary stress producers and even have devised a point system to determine if someone is overstressed. Certainly, having a child leave home falls into this category and may even include several personal changes.

The Mix

You can see how the letting-go process involves a mix of emotions. Actually, you probably have already experienced several of these—joy, sadness, pride, apprehension, and, certainly, love—as you've watched your son or daughter approach the end of his or her high school years.

While the roller coaster emotional ride has been both exhilarating and exhausting, it's not over yet. During the next few years, you will continue to hit those highs and lows. So be prepared, especially for the jolt at the end of the ride.

The Preparation

It helps to think through your emotions—how you might feel at specific times in the near and distant future and to imagine appropriate responses. For example, what will you feel and how should you respond at these moments? (Possible answers are in parentheses.)

- You read a story about something terrible happening to a young person far from home (fear/anxiety—pray and ask God to help you trust in his loving care for you and your child).

- You hear your child enthusiastically explain his or her plans to an adult friend (joy—affirm your son or daughter's excitement, and don't dampen the joy by mentioning your feelings of sadness).

- Tears come as you help your child pack (sorrow—don't make a big deal about it; instead, reaffirm your love and explain to your son or daughter that you are sad because you will miss him or her).

- You begin the long drive home, after dropping off your child in a distant city (grief—focus on the positive qualities of your child and the fact that he or she has made it successfully, this far in life, and thank God).

- You walk past the empty bedroom and see your child's trophies, pictures, and mementos (sadness—pray for your child, that he or she will continue to prosper in the new environment).

- You greet your child at his or her return (excitement—be careful not to smother your child, and don't expect former family patterns and roles to be followed).

- During vacation, you hear your child make strong and cynical statements about family, church, or government (irritation/anger—instead of reacting quickly, with sarcasm, listen intently and offer soft responses).

- You discover that your child has wasted money on a foolish purchase or by doing poorly in school (frustration/anger—calmly explain that the money flow will end soon if something similar occurs again).

- You learn that your child has made a very bad choice and is being disciplined by the authorities (disappointment/sadness—you share your feelings and allow your son or daughter to experience the consequences of his or her actions).

I'm sure you can think of other situations. While we can't be ready for every occurrence, thinking through many of the possibilities in advance will help.

Forward and back; ups and downs; good and bad days—the preparation process for letting go moves through time in one direction, but it doesn't cooperate quite as predictably when it comes to events, emotions, and energy. Once you have overcome a certain obstacle (like the idea that three weeks from today you will leave her at college), that doesn't mean the thoughts and emotions won't hit you again like the first time it occurred to you. So think through the process and your possible feelings and reactions, and be ready for the emotional ride.

STRESS POINTS

(over 12 months)

Death of spouse or child	100
Divorce	73
Pregnancy termination/miscarriage	72
Separation	65
Jail term	63
Death of close family member	63
Major illness or injury	53
Wedding	50
Dismissal at work	47
Pregnancy	44
Birth of a child	39
Death of close friend	37
Change of career paths	36
Foreclosure of mortgage or loan	30
Change in responsibilities at work (promotion or demotion)	30
Son or daughter leaving home	**29**
Life partner beginning or stopping work	27
New house or living arrangements	25
Trouble with the managers in your workplace	23
Difficulty getting to work/traffic/parking	20
Holiday more than one week in length	13
Christmas period	12
Minor violations of law (parking fines, speeding fines)	11

300+ points indicates an experience of very high to extremely high levels of stress. This person's ability to cope and manage future stress is dangerously low.

Adapted from a profile by Success Technologies Pty. Ltd. www.success.net.au.

CONVERSATIONS

When it comes to facing the facts and dealing with the mixed emotions of parenting, marriage partners often find themselves strangely at odds about what they are experiencing. A child's independence might provoke pride in one parent and anger in another. A gush of tears from a toddler may create an instant surge of guilt in one parent while his or her spouse laughs at the humor in the event.

Since mismatched feelings rise from the same circumstances, a wise couple spends time describing feelings and explaining reasons. When they make room for a wide range of feelings, giving each other permission to respond differently, parents usually discover that they have deep feelings in common. In other words, mixed emotions sometimes give way to powerful, shared feelings—a couple holding each other with fierce pride over a child's attitudes, actions, or achievements.

At this point in the process of letting go, use these discussion starters and questions to think through the process and unwind those mixed emotions:

1. What similarities do you see between your present and past "letting go" experiences with your child?

2. At each of the specific moments described in this chapter (going to school and getting the license), what did you learn about your child? What did you learn about yourself?

3. When have you felt yourself slipping into denial about this event? What brings you back to reality?

4. What have you been feeling recently concerning your child leaving home? What has been in your emotional stew?

5. What experiences or patterns in your upbringing or person-ality might be causing you to respond differently than your spouse?

6. What can you do to be better prepared for future emotional experiences related to letting go?

A pessimist sees the difficult in every opportunity; an optimist sees the opportunity in every difficulty.
—Sir Winston Churchill

Chapter 2

PREPARING FOR CHANGES AND CHALLENGES

Some people seem to love change and celebrate each one: new job, new church, new relationship, or new community.

Not me.

In my last year of junior high, my family moved to the other side of town. The new house was close enough so that I wouldn't be changing schools, just neighborhoods. Yet I remember after school the day after the move, walking back to the old house, now empty, and walking through it—as sort of a protest, I guess. I remember feeling so sad and lonely, almost lost.

Perhaps you can identify with that experience. Change can be unsettling and threatening, breeding insecurity, uneasiness, and fear. And make no mistake—having a child leave home involves change, big change! Regardless of the size of your family and the adjustments and growth along life's journey so far, you have enjoyed the company of this child for eighteen years. Together you have experienced highs, lows, victories, defeats, and growing pains. You have known this child for all of his or her young life, and you know him or her better than anyone else. Together you've survived early and middle adolescence and, recently, have become closer.

Soon that child will be leaving. So, yes, that's a huge change. Your family will never be the same. It's the end of an era. But it's also a new beginning.

Working Yourself Out of a Job

A significant change involves how parent and child relate. Over the life of the child, changes have occurred as the child has matured. With babies, for example, mothers and fathers have to do everything: feeding, changing, transporting, and so forth. The baby is totally dependent upon others for life.

Eventually, the child learns to walk, think, and talk, and he or she voices strong feelings and opinions. But although the parents allow some input from junior, they are still in charge and call the shots.

WHAT GOD SAYS ABOUT CHANGE

- "He will turn the hearts of the fathers to their children, and he will change disobedient minds to accept godly wisdom" (Luke 1:17b).
- "And I am convinced that nothing can ever separate us from his love. Death can't, and life can't. The angels can't, and the demons can't. Our fears for today, our worries about tomorrow, and even the powers of hell can't keep God's love away. Whether we are high above the sky or in the deepest ocean, nothing in all creation will ever be able to separate us from the love of God that is revealed in Christ Jesus our Lord" (Romans 8:38–39).
- "What this means is that those who become Christians become new persons. They are not the same anymore, for the old life is gone. A new life has begun!" (2 Corinthians 5:17).
- "And I am sure that God, who began the good work within you, will continue his work until it is finally finished on that day when Christ Jesus comes back again" (Philippians 1:6).
- "I know the one in whom I trust, and I am sure that he is able to guard what I have entrusted to him until the day of his return" (2 Timothy 1:12b).
- "I will never fail you. I will never forsake you" (Hebrews 13:5b).
- "Jesus Christ is the same yesterday, today, and forever" (Hebrews 13:8).

As the child moves into early adolescence, the parents move from "controlling" to "coaching," helping their young teen learn to make responsible decisions and learn from experiencing consequences.

Now Mom and Dad come to a turning point in the relationship. They won't be present or even in the vicinity to control or coach their late adolescent. Even as they consult with their graduate, he or she will usually make the final decision. It's quite a transition for both parent and child.

One of the difficulties in this transition involves "obedience" and "honor." God expects children to obey mother and father. It's commanded (Ephesians 6:1). This command applies to boys and girls under their parents' care. Obviously the situation changes when a child gets married or lives on his or her own and is self-sufficient. College marks a time of transition, sort of a halfway house on the way to adulthood. During these few years, the child still is under his or her parents' authority, but that begins to change, gradually, as he or she moves ever closer to graduation and total independence.

While God's command to obey parents has limits, this isn't the case with his command to honor them. Children should always honor their parents (Exodus 20:12; Ephesians 6:2), treating them with dignity and respect and caring for them in their old age. So although children soon won't have to obey, they never outgrow their responsibility to honor.

This change in relationship with a child can be tough for a parent to handle.

Suddenly we have a host of new questions, which can be very confusing. We can be confused by feelings and by roles.

As we just discussed, this is a time of mixed emotions. Many parents don't know what to do with their feelings, with their sense of loss and guilt.

One woman shared that her son caused her so much trouble in high school that she couldn't wait for him to leave. She felt guilty that

One of the goals of parenting is to work yourself out of a job. You really don't want to parent your children forever . . . do you? Sooner or later, your kids need to grow up, leave the nest, and start living independently and responsibly. Your kids need to be weaned—which has never been easy for either the weaner or the weanee.

Wayne Rice, *Cleared for Takeoff* (Lakeside, CA: Understanding Your Teenager, 2000), vi.

she wasn't feeling sad like many other parents and figured she must have been a poor mother. But she said that when her son came home from college, "he was different, better. I actually enjoyed having him around." Then, when he left again, she felt sad to see him go.

Parents also are confused by their changing roles, and they don't know how to act and react. It seemed a lot easier when the

DEALING WITH THE CHANGES

The following can help you successfully "let go":

- Build an adult relationship with your child through calls, e-mails, letters, and "care" packages. Let the child control the timing of these interactions to help maintain his or her sense of freedom.
- Focus on the things you enjoyed doing before your child left home. Don't add new commitments to fill the void left by your child's absence. Focus on yourself for a while or other members of your family.
- Don't feel guilty if your adjustment is different than other parents. Everyone is different. Each parent makes the adjustment in his or her own time.
- Work to keep your emotions under wraps when speaking with your child. If you burst into tears in every conversation, he or she may feel even worse about being away and may stop talking with you altogether!
- Try not to focus conversations on problems or uncertainties you're facing. Help your child focus on his or her new goals and activities.
- Limit any other major changes in your life for now. Sending a child off is enough of a shock. Changing jobs or moving to a new house could send everyone over the edge!

Minnesota Higher Education Services Offices (www.mheso.state.mn.us)

kids were in the house. Even during the turbulent junior high years and the push-for-independence senior high years, everyone knew who was in charge, who was the boss. After this departure, however, the kids no longer will live at home, at least for much of the year. Except in the military, they will operate as their own bosses, setting curfews, choosing entertainment and other leisure time activities, deciding when to get involved and when to decline, and managing their time and money.

Parents wonder where their lines of authority begin and end, how they should guide and direct their children's lives from a distance, and how they should act when the kids return home.

What should we do? How should we react? What does it mean to begin to treat my "child" like an adult? What's next? With all these new questions, no wonder some parents get confused. The most important question to answer, however, is simply, "How can we make it through this stage of life positively and successfully, retaining our sanity and not alienating our kids?"

MAKING THE BEST OF THEIR LAST DAYS AT HOME

Perhaps you have heard the story about the avid duck hunter who was in the market for a new bird dog. After much looking around, he was thrilled to find, and purchase, a dog that could actually walk on water to retrieve a duck. The hunter could scarcely believe his good fortune, but he was sure that none of his friends would ever believe him.

The man decided to bring a friend, a pessimist by nature, with him on the next hunting trip. As they waited in the blind, a flock of ducks flew by. The hunters fired, a duck fell, and the dog responded and jumped into the water. The dog didn't sink, however; instead, he ran across the surface of the lake to retrieve the duck, getting only his paws slightly wet. This continued all day; each time a duck would fall, the dog would run on the top of the water to retrieve it.

The pessimistic friend watched carefully. He saw everything

but didn't say anything. On the way home, the hunter asked his friend if he had noticed anything different about his new dog.

"Yes, I sure did," answered the pessimist. "He can't swim."

Do you tend to be an optimist or a pessimist? Is the glass half full or half empty? At this stage of life, and at this point in the book, you may be experiencing some of the emotional upheaval that we have discussed and thinking about the challenges to come as your child sets sail, away from your shore.

But don't despair; there's another way to look at the situation. Yes, you will struggle, at times during the next few months and years, journeying through valleys and climbing mountains—it won't be easy. But, if you're looking closer, you'll also discover that this is the land of opportunity. I'm not encouraging you to ignore the problems or gloss over them with a sort of Pollyanna, "best of all possible worlds" attitude (I really don't think your dog will be able to walk on water). Denying reality doesn't help anyone. But focusing on the negative isn't very helpful either.

So let's see this parenting passage for what it is realistically and deal with the issues. And let's look for what God may be teaching us and for the opportunities that he gives. We need to make the most of the time we have left—before they leave.

Making the most of our time affects directly how we relate to our spouses and children. Daily we rush from responsibilities at work to those at home and at church, hustling and bustling, fighting traffic, paying bills, meeting deadlines, doing good, and probably helping many people—perhaps, even, doing "the Lord's work." But in the process, I'm afraid we often move right past those closest to us who need us the most. And then, when it's too late, we look back with regret, realizing that our priorities, our values, were out of whack. As Paul Tsongas once remarked, "No one ever said on his deathbed, 'I wish I had spent more time in the office'" (quoted by Anne Quindlen in her Villanova commencement address: www.aboutschool.com/graduation.htm). Our spouses need us. Our children need us. Let's figure out how to spend quantity and quality time with them in the years we have left.

Parent to Child

Because the son or daughter has graduated and is moving quickly toward independence, parents may think that he or she is pushing for autonomy even sooner than expected. This can be a source of real conflict between the child and the parents. One mom recently shared that the summer before leaving for college her demure, sweet, calm, and compliant daughter became a real pain. "It was as though she was trying to make the separation easier for me. She was so obnoxious at times that I was almost glad to see her go! Then I felt guilty for having those feelings."

So even though you will feel this way occasionally, resist the temptation to blurt out something like, "I'm glad you're leaving!" (That will just add to your guilty feelings.)

A good principle to remember here is act, don't react. In other words, take the initiative, be proactive. You could, for example, explain to your son or daughter that you share the same goal. You both want him or her to be a mature, autonomous adult, living on his or her own, away from your supervision. You and your child may have different approaches for getting there, but your goal is the same. At least you can agree on that.

You also could encourage the child not to take everything you say or do in the next few weeks as deliberate efforts to hurt him or her. You really do want nothing but the best for your son or daughter. Your motive is love.

Adult to Adult

You hope, eventually, to enjoy a peer-to-peer relationship with your child. You always will be the parent, of course, but your relationship should mature to adult-to-adult rather than parent-to-child. Hopefully you'll get there in a few years. But the transition may be brutal, as you and your child bounce back and forth between roles.

Thus, to deepen your relationship with this son or daughter, you should begin treating him or her like a friend. By this I mean acting as though your child is more like an adult friend than the little boy or girl whose pictures adorn your tables and walls. You can do this in various ways. Here's a suggestion: have fun together.

Before your late adolescent leaves, do one or two adult activities together that he or she would like to do. Did you catch that? The activities should be those that your child would enjoy. And be sure to repeat those and add others in the future when he or she is home on vacation or military leave. These adult activities can be as simple as having lunch at a restaurant or going shopping. Or you might want to attend a concert or professional sporting event together.

I have seen fathers bring their college-age sons to men's breakfasts and retreats, and I've heard of mothers who have brought their daughters to women's Bible studies and luncheons. At church, invite your son or daughter to accompany you to an adult class (or assist him or her in choosing one). In other words, help your graduate move away from high school and into the adult world.

LIVING WITH NO REGRETS

Mike Swider is a tough-as-nails football coach. He's also an outstanding athlete in his own right. A few years ago, while competing in a triathlon, he saw a competitor wearing a T-shirt with the statement "Don't die wondering!" The clear message is to live now so that when you come to the end of life, you'll have no regrets. You won't be thinking, "I wonder if . . . ," "I wish I had . . . ," or "If only I had . . ."

Mike has taken "Don't die wondering" as a personal challenge, and he shares it with his team each year. His message is, "Leave it all on the field. Play the game with no regrets." And he encourages them to live that way as well.

I can think of no better challenge for us parents, to live with no regrets. It certainly is the best way to prepare for the changes and challenges ahead. And it begins by doing what we know we should, now.

No Wondering . . . No Regrets

Too often, however, parents reach this point of releasing the child, filled with "wondering." Mixed with our grief is a measure of regret, looking back and considering what we might have done better in rearing our children and in preparing them for life on their own in the world. Many parents feel tremendous guilt as they reflect on the past and wonder where the time went:

- The father who was always out of town and missed many of his son's school activities and games

- The mother whose time was consumed by the smaller children causing her to neglect her older daughter

- The couple who always seemed to be arguing about money

- The Christian worker who invested time in the ministry and ignored the family

These parents all had good intentions about changing their lifestyles, but time slipped past and now it's too late. They grieve their lost opportunities.

Here's a bulletin: You can't do anything about the past; it's gone. But you can do something about the present. So begin now, today, to live with no regrets.

During her daughter's junior year in high school, Mitzie Barton would sit in the stands with other moms and dads, watching her daughter, Kari, play basketball. As she spoke with the parents of seniors on the team, the talk would often turn to their feelings and what they were doing to prepare themselves for the trauma of their daughters leaving home. "Practice going by the empty bedroom" and "Don't miss anything—games, programs, dates—so you'll have no regrets," they advised. Mitzie explains, "So I didn't! I worked hard at being there because I didn't want to look back and think, 'I wish I had done more.'"

Forgive . . . No Regrets

Another important step in living without regrets is to release the past—to move on with our lives. No one is perfect (a problem for us perfectionists), and we all have 20/20 hindsight. So we can easily fall into rehearsing past actions and outcomes. But that's a counterproductive and even destructive practice.

Certainly mistakes have been made, hateful words have been spoken, poor actions have been taken, and wrong directions have been chosen, by you and by your child. But that's "before," and now you're living in the "after." It's over and done. Let it go. See this as an opportunity to make a fresh start.

Some parents use the past as a weapon, constantly reminding children of their mistakes. They may verbally batter them with declarations like these:

- "I told you to take biology. Now you'll never get into pre-med."

- "Just think—you could have married Michael; look what he's done with his life!"

- "When I think of those wasted years in high school, I just want to cry."

GOD'S WORD ON FORGIVING AND FORGETTING

- "You are a God of forgiveness, gracious and merciful, slow to become angry, and full of unfailing love and mercy. You did not abandon them" (Nehemiah 9:17b).
- "O Lord, you are so good, so ready to forgive, so full of unfailing love for all who ask your aid" (Psalm 86:5).
- "So he returned home to his father. And while he was still a long distance away, his father saw him coming. Filled with love and compassion, he ran to his son, embraced him, and kissed him. His son said to him, 'Father, I have sinned against both heaven and you, and I am no longer worthy of being called your son.'
  "But his father said to the servants, 'Quick! Bring the finest robe in the house and put it on him. Get a ring for his finger, and sandals for his feet. And kill the calf we have been fattening in the pen. We must celebrate with a feast, for this son of mine was dead and has now returned to life. He was lost, but now he is found.' So the party began" (Luke 15:20–24).
- "If you forgive those who sin against you, your heavenly Father will forgive you. But if you refuse to forgive others, your Father will not forgive your sins" (Matthew 6:14–15).
- "Even if he wrongs you seven times a day and each time turns again and asks forgiveness, forgive him" (Luke 17:4).
- "I am focusing all my energies on this one thing: Forgetting the past and looking forward to what lies ahead, I strain to reach the end of the race and receive the prize for which God, through Christ Jesus, is calling us up to heaven" (Philippians 3:13b–14).
- "Since you have been raised to new life with Christ, set your sights on the realities of heaven, where Christ sits at God's right hand in the place of honor and power" (Colossians 3:1).

- "If you had worked harder and hustled more, you could have had that scholarship."

And, as mentioned earlier, some parents beat themselves up with the past, constantly reviewing and reliving crucial moments or lost opportunities with thoughts such as these:

- "I shouldn't have pushed him so hard."

- "If only we hadn't moved!"

- "Time passes so quickly. We just didn't spend enough time together, and now she's gone!"

- "It's my fault. He is just like me!"

Whether or not those statements are true is irrelevant. We need to forgive our children and ourselves and move forward. We need to pray, as did David, "Create in me a clean heart, O God. Renew a right spirit within me. . . . Restore to me again the joy of your salvation, and make me willing to obey you" (Psalm 51:10, 12). Then we need to let it go.

Be prepared!

CONVERSATIONS

Changes are coming, whether or not you are ready for them. Use these questions to help you prepare for all of them and the accompanying challenges.

1. Was it easy or difficult for your parents to "release" you? How do you know?

2. Why do you find it difficult to trust your middle or late adolescent? When you try to control him or her, what tactics do you use?

3. What does the phrase "working yourself out of a job" mean to you? What can you do to make that happen?

4. What are you doing to make the most of your child's last days at home? What will you be doing?

5. What is hard to forgive in your child? In yourself?

6. Living with no regrets isn't easy. What will it take for you
    to be able to release your son or daughter with no regrets?

As parents, we have to offer the best we can. But the scary part is not knowing if or when our kids will ever make it their own!
—Neil Wilson

Chapter 3

LIVING "ON MY OWN"—IS YOUR TEEN READY?

Recovery groups have long used a version of Reinhold Niebuhr's "Serenity Prayer": God grant me the serenity to accept the things I cannot change, the courage to change the things I can, and the wisdom to know the difference. This prayer has profound implications for parents, especially as they watch their children grow, mature, and leave home. In the last chapter, we saw that by nature we resist changes and new beginnings, especially when life is going well. Change makes us nervous and insecure. Yet during this time of transition, our families, our high school graduates, and our parent-child relationships are changing considerably. These alterations are real; there's no denying it.

Some changes we need to accept—so we need serenity. Some changes we need to make—so we need courage. But most of all, we need wisdom to know the difference.

RELEASE

Perhaps the biggest reality at this point in your parenting experience is the fact that your child is crossing the threshold into adulthood. Right now, he or she is in the process of leaving forever the stage of life as your little boy or girl. Having the serenity to accept this truth means loosening your grasp and releasing your son or daughter to become an autonomous and mature adult.

Stu Weber writes:

> One of the things we need to restore is a sense of release, a moment in time when everybody involved in our child's life realizes, "This young person is now responsible for his or her own life." That can come in any number of ways. With my own parents, it wasn't a formal event at all. It was a moment none of us would have or could have rehearsed. I don't know how deliberate or practiced it was, but I do remember it as vividly now as the day it happened. It took place at a train depot. I was off for college. For the first time in my life

I was leaving home for an extended season. I saw it in their eyes. It was strong. It was an unforgettable moment. In later years, my mother would say that from that moment on, it was never the same. It was more than getting on a train for Illinois. It was leaving childhood. (Stu Weber, *Tender Warrior: God's Intention for a Man* (Sisters, Ore: Multnomah Books, 1993), 166)

Control or Trust?

Releasing is difficult if we tend to be controlling in our relationships, especially in our families. Too often parents try to control their adult children. They can't do it physically anymore, so they may use money (can you say "bribery"?), pressure, fear, and guilt (a biggie). This happens beyond the home as well. If you've ever been on the receiving end of those attempts—in business, at church, in the community, or in the family—you know how frustrated you can feel. Eventually, you try to avoid people who employ such tactics, or, as in the case of family members, you dread and then simply endure your time together. So think about it—is that how you want your kids to feel about you? Probably not.

In reality, the "control" these people think they exert is illusory, especially with older children. That is, parents may think they're controlling the behavior of their late adolescent or adult offspring, but whatever control they have lasts only as long as those parents and their children are together. As soon as they are away from Mom and Dad, these young men and women resume living as they please. Sometimes they may even intentionally do, away from home, just what their parents forbade in their presence.

Consider recent high school graduates in that situation. No matter what their mothers and fathers tell, pressure, or order them to do or to not do, when the graduates are out of their parents' sight and direct influence, they have the freedom to do just the opposite. That's a scary thought, right? But here's the good news. If we have modeled the right values, taught life skills, and allowed them increasing opportunities to make decisions as they've matured, they probably will do what is right on their own, out of our sight.

That's not guaranteed, of course. But it's where trust comes in. Do we offer counsel? Sure. Do we express concern when appropriate? You bet. Do we pray a lot? No question about it.

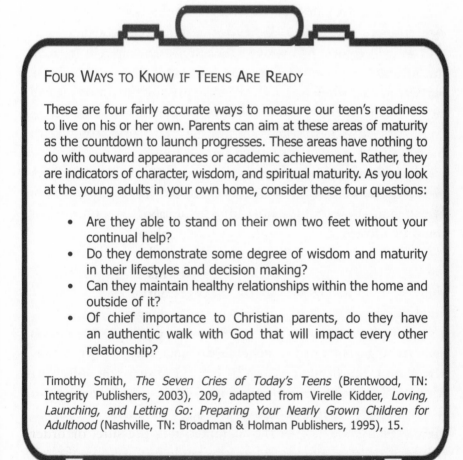

FOUR WAYS TO KNOW IF TEENS ARE READY

These are four fairly accurate ways to measure our teen's readiness to live on his or her own. Parents can aim at these areas of maturity as the countdown to launch progresses. These areas have nothing to do with outward appearances or academic achievement. Rather, they are indicators of character, wisdom, and spiritual maturity. As you look at the young adults in your own home, consider these four questions:

- Are they able to stand on their own two feet without your continual help?
- Do they demonstrate some degree of wisdom and maturity in their lifestyles and decision making?
- Can they maintain healthy relationships within the home and outside of it?
- Of chief importance to Christian parents, do they have an authentic walk with God that will impact every other relationship?

Timothy Smith, *The Seven Cries of Today's Teens* (Brentwood, TN: Integrity Publishers, 2003), 209, adapted from Virelle Kidder, *Loving, Launching, and Letting Go: Preparing Your Nearly Grown Children for Adulthood* (Nashville, TN: Broadman & Holman Publishers, 1995), 15.

But in the end, we need to trust God and trust our kids. Actually, we don't have any other choice.

True release means trust, not control.

Risk

Release always comes with risk. That's a fact of life with which we're all too familiar. When we loan something to a friend, the risk is that he or she may not bring it back. When we drop a letter in the mailbox, the risk is that the letter will be lost. When we invest money in the stock market, the risk is that the stocks will fail and we'll lose our investment. When we perform publicly, the risk is that we will receive bad reviews. When we confide to a friend a precious dream, fear, or failure, the risk is that the friend will leak our secret. And when we let go of a child, we risk that he or she will go the wrong direction.

Whatever we have released is just out there, away from us. It's risky business. No wonder letting go is so tough.

Even though this will be difficult, we must turn the corner mentally and take that risk. And we need to agree with our sons or daughters that they are now adults and largely responsible for their own lives.

TRAITS OF RESPONSIBLE ADULTS

Hopefully, your children will know how a responsible adult acts by watching you. On the other hand, regardless of what they catch from your lifestyle, it will be helpful to share the following list with them at an appropriate time. You may also want to print it out and give it to your graduate (after your talk, of course). Here's the list; we'll cover the characteristics one at a time.

Responsible adults

- make carefully considered decisions;

- follow a moral compass;

- take responsibility for their actions;

- show consideration for others;

- help those in need;

- speak and live the truth;

- pay their own way;

- invest their resources wisely;

- take good care of what has been entrusted to them;

- live in the present with an eye on the future.

Now let's take a closer look.

Responsible Adults Make Carefully Considered Decisions

Hopefully you have already taught your child decision-making skills, especially as you have thought through this next step in life (for example, deciding which college to attend). If not, this would be a good time. Explain that they will see many of their new friends acting impetuously and making foolish decisions. Recently, for example, in a nearby community, three high school friends decided to pull a prank and steal a security golf cart from their school and drive it to a nearby park. A custodian saw them and called the police. One of the police officers, who responded to the call and was chasing the teens, collapsed and died of an apparent heart attack. So something that seemed like fun, a spur-of-the-moment decision, turned tragic.

Unfortunately, our news is littered with other examples of people (not just young people under the influence of alcohol) making bad decisions and doing stupid things.

Responsible adults, in contrast, think through the possible consequences of their actions. They also consider the costs and other factors. Then they make well-reasoned decisions.

Responsible Adults Follow a Moral Compass

A popular philosophy these days seems to be "do whatever you want—whatever feels good." Your son or daughter, away from your supervision and restraints and the watchful eyes of adult friends and neighbors, will be tempted to go that direction, especially when many of those around them do. But they've watched you and know your morality and values. As Christians who read their Bible, they also know right from wrong.

So at this point, simply remind your son or daughter to follow that compass. And reassure him or her of your trust.

Responsible Adults Take Responsibility for Their Actions

It's human nature to shift the blame. Check out the first few chapters of Genesis where Adam and Eve rationalized their disobedience. And since then, we always seem to be looking for excuses for our mistakes and sins: "It's not my fault!" "I forgot." "Who can blame me after what I'm going through?" "I lost it in the sun!" Remember the last time you were stopped for speeding? What was your excuse? What did you say to the officer to try to get out of the ticket? And then if you were honest with yourself, you had to admit that for whatever reason, you were driving over the speed limit and deserved the fine.

It takes a mature man or woman to own up to his or her actions and to accept the consequences. Yet that's the mark of a responsible adult. So explain to your graduate that you don't expect perfection; you know mistakes will be made. But you do expect him or her to face the truth, accept the truth, and own up to his or her mistakes.

Responsible Adults Show Consideration for Others

For most of your child's existence, life has revolved around him or her. That's natural, of course, and nothing to feel guilty about. We certainly wouldn't expect an infant or small child to fend for him-or herself and to serve others. Yet as they grow and mature, children should learn that others have needs as well, that life is not all about them. We know that many adults still haven't learned this lesson and are very self-centered. But responsible adults are considerate.

This is an important lesson to learn when dealing with a roommate and others with whom your graduate will live, work, and study. In effect, it means living out the Golden Rule (Matthew 7:12). And this leads us to the next characteristic.

Responsible Adults Help Those in Need

Continuing with the theme of "it's not all about you," we see that responsible, Christian adults look for ways to serve others, especially those who are hurting. When Jesus washed the disciples' feet, he said, "Do you understand what I was doing? You call me 'Teacher' and 'Lord,' and you are right, because it is true. And since I, the Lord and Teacher, have washed your feet, you ought to wash each other's feet. I have given you an example to follow. Do as I have done to you. How true it is that a servant is not greater than the master. Nor are messengers more important

I tossed restlessly as the wind whistled through the trees outside my bedroom window, surprised by my sleeplessness. I thought of my son and daughter, finally settled in college dormitories on opposite ends of the continent. It had been a long, wearying journey getting them this far, so why couldn't I sleep?

I got up and went into their rooms, banishing the silence with a flurry of shaking, dusting, and sweeping, stopping now and then to examine the discards of their childhood—outgrown clothes, old term papers, even, in a corner, a tattered teddy bear. It had always comforted me, that annual autumn rite, as if by changing the linen on their beds and lining their bureau drawers, I was making a fresh start for them. But that night the familiar tasks seemed futile. I was troubled by the idea that there was some essential parental task I had neglected, like taking them to the dentist or teaching them to say "please" and "thank you." But their teeth and their manners were sound, so it could not be that. And it occurred to me that I was refurbishing and repairing a past they had already put behind them—that although they would be returning to this house, to these rooms, they would not be living in them again, merely passing through. And that whatever I forgot to do for them—to teach, show, notice, praise, give, or honor—they must do for themselves, or else do without. And that was why I could not sleep.

Jane Adams, "Whose Life Is It Anyway?" *Good Housekeeping* (February, 1994): 62, an excerpt from, *I'm Still Your Mother: How to Get Along with Your Grown-Up Children for the Rest of Your Life* (New York: Delacorte Press, 1994).

than the one who sends them. You know these things—now do them! That is the path of blessing" (John 13:12–17).

This is also counter-cultural, although many young people are incredible models of selfless service. If your child has traveled with the youth group in a missions trip, then he or she has practiced selfless service.

Responsible Adults Speak and Live the Truth

As Christians, we believe that truth, absolute truth, exists. Jesus said, "I am the way, the truth, and the life. No one can come to the Father except through me" (John 14:6). He is the Truth. We also believe that the Bible is true; that is, Scripture is the inerrant and infallible Word of God.

So we are people of truth. But we must also live what we say we believe. And responsible adults, especially Christian adults, refuse to lie, even if it means accepting painful consequences for their actions. Being truthful includes being reliable too; that is, people should know they can believe us and count on us to keep our word. So encourage your graduate to tell the truth, to friends, teachers, employers, and other adults, and to you (you can handle it).

Responsible Adults Pay Their Own Way

In other words, they don't mooch off others. I remember a college friend who had a car on campus when most of those in his class didn't. One day he told me that he was about ready to take the car home and leave it there because of all the hassles. Everyone, it seemed, wanted to use his car (without putting any gas in it) or wanted him to drive them somewhere.

Explain that the world has "givers" and "takers." Then encourage your child to not get the reputation as a "taker," always asking for something, never picking up the tab, or not paying his or her fair share.

And this leads to the next two characteristics, both of which concern the biblical principle of stewardship.

Responsible Adults Invest Their Resources Wisely and Take Good Care of What Has Been Entrusted to Them

In other words, they don't waste money or make foolish purchases. "Resources" also include time, talents, and possessions. As Christians, we believe that God has entrusted us with much that he expects us to use wisely, investing for kingdom purposes (see Matthew 25:19–21).

If your graduate is going to college, explain that this is an opportunity that many in the world don't have. Encourage your son or daughter to see the time spent at the institution of higher education as an investment in his or her life and that the total experience—educationally, socially, physically, emotionally, and spiritually—will build a solid foundation for making a difference for Christ in the world. In other words, going off to college is not just about getting away from home and having fun with other recently released adolescents.

Responsible Adults Live in the Present with an Eye on the Future

Some people live in the past and are always talking about the "good old days." This practice isn't limited to older folks. Your child will encounter young people who seem to have reached their peak in high school. Back there, in their hometown and on that campus, they had status as members of the "in crowd" and had all their needs met by Mom and Dad. These students continually refer back to the good times.

Some people live in the future; that is, they believe that some day they will find happiness, romance, fulfillment, and wealth, that their "ship will come in." They may not be doing much today, but eventually they will.

> For me, the most difficult part of letting go was releasing my daughter to do what we had been preparing her to do—to make decisions on her own.
>
> Jim Burns

People of both these types find it difficult to be happy or content with where they are now, with the present.

In contrast, your son or daughter will probably encounter many who seem to only live for the moment. They want to party hardy, regardless of the future consequences. Their motto seems to be "live for today because we could be dead tomorrow." And, sadly, many throw away their futures for the present.

Responsible adults, however, seize the moment but also realize that their present actions have future consequences. So encourage your graduate to enjoy every day of this life away from you and your restrictions and watchfulness, but to do so responsibly, understanding the future ramifications of his or her actions.

What to Teach Your Child Before He or She Leaves Home

We've already touched on a number of issues that should be covered before the child heads off on his or her own. But here are some specific and practical matters to discuss and teach.

Practical Information

Remember this important principle: *we model values and teach skills.*

Actually, we cannot *not* model values. People, especially those who live with us, learn what we value by watching us. We show

how much we value something, how important it is to us, by how we invest our time, money, and emotion.

My family, for example, can tell very quickly that I value my new running shoes much more than my old, worn-out ones that I throw in the corner of the garage and wear when I do yard work. Sometimes, our actions belie our statements. For example, I can say that my children are important to me, but if I travel all the time and ignore them when I'm home, I'm preaching the opposite message.

And here's a disturbing truth: your children will catch your values.

Not all family values are good . . . I'm proposing that we shape our family cultures, systematically thinking them through, strengthening what has value and changing what does not.

To help do that, I've gone through the Bible looking for core values . . . I came up with fourteen:

1. God first
2. Concern for others
3. Hard work
4. Truthfulness
5. Generosity
6. Submission
7. Sexual fidelity
8. Family unity and love
9. Boundaries
10. Joy and thanksgiving
11. Rest
12. Care for creation
13. Contentment
14. Grace

Tim Stafford, *Never Mind the Joneses: Building Core Christian Values in a Way That Fits Your Family* (Downers Grove, IL: InterVarsity Press, 2004), 24–26.

Even if they seem to swing away from them for a time during the first few years away from home, usually they eventually swing back, for better or worse. So, hopefully, your child has caught positive values from watching you live.

But notice the second half of that principle: we teach skills. In other words, if we want our kids to learn life skills, we have to be intentional—we have to teach. Take the matter of tying shoes, for example. We can model that exercise all we want, but our children won't learn how to tie their shoes by watching. Instead, we have to teach them, step by step.

Use these steps to teach a skill:

- Explain: You tell what has to be done.

- Demonstrate: You show what has to be done by doing it.

- Supervise: Your child does the skill under your direction, and you offer correction when needed.

- Affirm: Your child does the skill on his or her own, returning for advice. You troubleshoot and affirm, correcting what was wrong and praising what was right.

Another way to describe those steps is *tell*, *show*, *do*, and *go*.

So what skills should our children know before heading away from home and on their own? Here are a few:

- How to survive and thrive spiritually

- How to study the Bible

- How to wash clothes

- How to iron clothes

- How to budget money

- How to get along with a roommate

- How to resolve conflict

- How to make a decision

- How to handle a crisis

- How to be organized

- How to schedule time

- How to get things done

- How to develop healthy eating, sleeping, and exercising habits

You probably can add others. In addition, while not strictly skills like those above, you should cover how to find a church, how to avoid the freshman twenty (the weight often put on during freshman year), and other similar lessons.

Teach a couple of these skills at a time, over a month or two before your child leaves. Just be sure to give him or her time to practice the skills independently when you can observe his or her success (the "affirm" step).

Biblical Information

The Bible is very clear about the power of God's Word (Psalm 119:11; 2 Timothy 3:16; Hebrews 4:12). It just makes sense, therefore, to read it, study it, memorize it, and apply it. Scripture should be in our hearts and lives.

Thus, I offer Bible passages for the journey—verses that every graduate should know. They're printed in canonical order in the Appendix.

And here's a thought: work on memorizing them together. It will bless both of you.

An aspect that was difficult was the reflection in our hearts and spirits about "What did we forget to teach them? Have we done all that God needed us to do to equip them?" Of course the answer is no, but we did just what we knew to do with the tools and time we had.

My mom called recently with a quickened heart and voice and shared, "Gary, I was speaking to some of my girlfriends over a game of bridge and was horrified over something I forgot to teach you."

"Mom, what could you have forgotten?" I asked.

"I never taught you how to floss your teeth. Did you ever learn?"

I laughed and still do over that experience. I recall saying, "Mom, if that is all you are worried about at eighty-four years of age and the only regret you have, you did good, girl. You did well!"

Gary Rosberg

WHAT TO DO TO MAKE YOUR CHILD'S INDEPENDENCE SUCCESSFUL

Our kids may not believe this statement, especially during the teenage years, but it's true: we want the same thing that they want—for them to be independent of us, autonomous, grown-up, on their own. It's just that the transition to that stage of life can be a bit bumpy. So let your child know that you are cheering for him or her to succeed.

But to help your child successfully transition to independence from you, here are a couple of cautions.

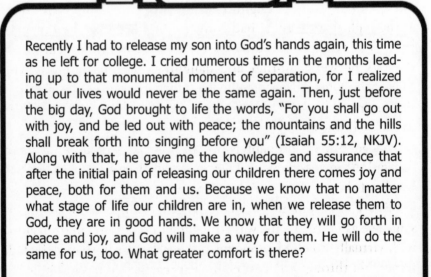

Recently I had to release my son into God's hands again, this time as he left for college. I cried numerous times in the months leading up to that monumental moment of separation, for I realized that our lives would never be the same again. Then, just before the big day, God brought to life the words, "For you shall go out with joy, and be led out with peace; the mountains and the hills shall break forth into singing before you" (Isaiah 55:12, NKJV). Along with that, he gave me the knowledge and assurance that after the initial pain of releasing our children there comes joy and peace, both for them and us. Because we know that no matter what stage of life our children are in, when we release them to God, they are in good hands. We know that they will go forth in peace and joy, and God will make a way for them. He will do the same for us, too. What greater comfort is there?

Stormie Omartian, *The Power of a Praying Parent* (Eugene, OR: Harvest House Publishers, 1995), 32.

Caution #1: Don't Burden Your Child with Your Emotions

One of those bumps on the transition road can be caused by the mix of our emotions: joy, sadness, guilt, hope, and fear. Parents are happy for their kids and hopeful for their future, but they are fearful too. And they can't help but wonder if the kids were ready for this big step in their lives: Will they go to church? Will they say no to premarital sex? Are they self-disciplined enough to get up, go to class, and study on their own? Will they find friends? Will they be happy? Will they be safe? When will I see them again? With all those legitimate emotions and questions swirling, we can be tempted to lay them on our kids. For example, some parents, usually unintentionally, make their children feel guilty for growing up.

Doris, a single mom, struggled with the thought of her daughter, an only child, leaving home and leaving her alone. I knew Doris and her daughter, Ann, through the music program at the high school, and I had conversed with them often through the years. While I certainly wasn't in their home to hear any of the talk between mother and daughter on this topic, knowing Doris, I can imagine what she probably said when they spoke of the future. During Ann's senior year, I remember asking what she would be doing after graduation. She answered, "I'd really like to go to college, but I'll probably work and take classes at [local junior college]. Mom needs me." That was eight years ago, and she still hasn't left home. Ann can't break away.

But I also remember Diane, another single mom about the same age as Doris. Diane was struggling to rear four children alone, with virtually no child support from her former husband, the kids' father. Yet through the past eight years each child has left home, in turn, and two have since graduated from college. Again, I wasn't privy to those private family conversations, but clearly Diane had it right. I know she struggled emotionally when each child left home, but she didn't use her sorrow as leverage to make them stay.

Sharing your feelings of sadness with your child is fine, but balance this out by sharing your joy and excitement as well. You could say something like this: "You've probably noticed that I've gotten a bit misty-eyed lately, and I have to warn you, it's just going to get worse. I'll probably be a blubbering idiot! [laugh] It's not easy being a parent and watching my wonderful child grow up and leave home. I love you so much, and you know I'm going to miss you. So bear with me. But I also want you to know how happy I am at the same time. This is such an exciting moment for us as a family—we're all so proud of you. And you're going to have a ball next year—I just know it!"

Take the same approach with your fears. You can share your concerns with your child, admitting that worrying comes with the job description for parents. But also explain how you are trusting God to care for him or her.

Caution #2: Don't Burden Your Child with Your Dreams

One of the facts of parenting is that our children seldom live up to our idealistic dreams for them when they were very young. This makes it tough to accept the reality of who they are now.

Jeremy casts an imposing shadow on the athletic field. At six foot six and 240 pounds, he can scan the secondary and choose the open receiver to hit with a short bullet pass or soft, arching, deep toss. When his pass protection breaks down, Jeremy can scramble out of trouble. Unusually quick and agile for his size, he outruns most of the backs during practice and has emerged as the second-leading rusher on the team. Already colleges have been scouting this talented sophomore.

After football, Jeremy plays power forward on the varsity basketball team and has been touted by local newspapers as a possible all-state selection. In the spring, Jeremy plays first base, although it is rumored that he may not be playing baseball this

spring. Instead, he prob-
ably will garner the
romantic lead in the
school musical. Jeremy's
first love is music: he
sings first tenor in the a
cappella choir and plays
a mean sax in the jazz
ensemble.

> Some parents are so impressed with their kids that they don't give guidance. Others are so depressed that they don't give encouragement. Don't write your kids off or give up. Keep guiding, encouraging, and loving them.
>
> Bruce Barton

In addition to his
activities at West High, Jeremy volunteers at a local nursing
home, helps lead his church youth group, and actively partici-
pates in Campus Life. Jeremy is known for his strong Christian
commitment.

With all of these activities and responsibilities, you might
expect Jeremy's grades to suffer. But he carries a full schedule of
honors courses and all A's on his report cards. In addition, he serves
as sophomore class president and will be the school's representative
to Boys' State.

If you think Jeremy is too good to be true, you're right—I made
him up. But he matches what many parents imagine and dream for
their sons. A daughter's scenario would be similar—outstanding in
athletics, academics, and student government, homecoming queen,
spiritual giant, popular, beautiful, and talented in art, dance,
music, and drama. Other parents may dream beyond high school:
Olympics, a doctor, star of stage and screen, the president of the
United States.

As we rock our newborns to sleep, we wonder what they will
be . . . and we dream.

We know, of course, that not all of those dreams are possible,
and we're willing to settle for less. But deep in our hearts we
know that this child will be something special!

Truthfully, each child *is* special—a unique creation of our
loving God and packed with his or her own blend of talents,
gifts, abilities, and potential. The problem, however, is that the

child may not match the picture in the minds of his or her parents. That can lead to conflicts and feelings of disappointment. One day the parents will have to adjust their dreams to match reality.

For children in the crib and in our arms, dreams come easily. But as our babies begin to grow, interact with other children, and go to school, the ideals meet reality. Parents' dream adjustments come in stages throughout the parenting process, but often they peak during the high school or college years. And the experience of coming to grips with what their kids are becoming can be a struggle and may catch them by surprise.

Often this happens during this time of letting go. Releasing them from our dreams and ideals can be painfully difficult.

Actually, you may find that you have to make a series of mid-course corrections—releases—in the next few years. When my friend's son was in high school, he planned on becoming an aerospace engineer. And you can imagine the proud father sharing this news with friends and neighbors. During his sophomore year at a Christian college, however, the boy changed his major to Christian education. I knew this had to be tough for his parents (especially his dad) to accept. They had nothing against the major and even had a person on their church staff that had majored in Christian education; yet, their dream for their son was something quite different. I learned a lesson from that godly couple as they accepted their son's decision with grace and affirmation. I need to add that he changed majors and careers a few more times since then!

So as your child makes this transition to independence, be part of the solution, not the problem.

GETTING READY TO LET THEM LIVE ON THEIR OWN

Here's an important question: are you ready? You may not feel like it with all the emotions and issues and with the hours and days passing so quickly. Many parents spend an inordinate amount of time worrying about what will happen to them and their children. They can even become paralyzed by anxiety.

The antidote is trust—in God and his faithfulness. He was there for you in the past; he's with you now; he will be with you in the future.

When we get to this point in our earthly journey and in the lives of our children, we tend to reflect, to think back to memorable and defining moments. Quite frankly, at times in the past we wondered if we'd ever get to this age, to this place, to this parenting passage.

Some of us struggled with having children and doubted that we would even become parents. But God intervened, and we did. And that was the first miracle.

Even if you were one of those who found getting pregnant and carrying the baby to term relatively easy, the birth of that first child was just the beginning of a series of miracles in your lives together. And all parents can think back and remember the sicknesses and injuries, the sleepless nights, the stress and worries, and our frantic prayers—times when we even wondered about survival, but we made it.

Our parenting journey took us over hills and through valleys; yet at each step along the way, God was with us—guiding, comforting, leading, and assuring. Many times we believed we had control; at least we acted as though that were true. But then, circumstances exposed our finiteness, and we realized that the only one in control was God.

So how should the reality of God's faithfulness in the past impact us today? With an outpouring of gratitude and joy. We should use this occasion of our child's leaving home as a signpost, a monument to the continual care of our powerful and loving Lord. That's the best way to get ready, to prepare. Thanking God for what he has done, we should eagerly look forward to his future blessings in our lives and in the lives of our children.

CONVERSATIONS

When we look at our growing and maturing young person, often we still see him or her as a child. Yet this child is an emerging adult and soon will live on his or her own. Thus both parent and child need to be ready for this new stage in life.

1. How is your child adjusting to this approaching new era in his or her life? What signs of maturity have you seen so far?

2. Which of your values do you see replicated in your child?

3. Which of the skills listed do you still need to teach your son or daughter? What is your plan for doing that?

4. Of all those verses listed (in the Appendix), which one or two have proven most meaningful to you over the years? Which ones do you think will be most helpful to your son or daughter in the next year or two? Why?

5. When have you been tempted to burden your child with your emotions or dreams? What can you do to make sure that you don't?

6. What evidence from the past do you have of God's faithfulness? How will those reminders help you at this time in your life?

*Watching one of my
kids grow up and fly
away is like cutting
off one of my limbs.*
—John Ortberg

Chapter 4

GETTING THE
MOST OUT
OF THE DAY
THEY LEAVE

Some kids are so ready to leave and to begin this next exciting time of life that they almost push their parents toward the car and the trip home. While these moms and dads are waiting for the warm good-byes, the kids say, in effect, "We have friends here and stuff to do . . . so we'll see you." They can't wait to begin this new stage in their lives, away from home and making decisions for themselves. Conversely, some grads find the pending separation difficult, and although they probably won't show it at the time, they grieve nearly as much as their parents.

Mitzie Barton had listened carefully to other parents who were going through the letting-go process and had tried to follow their advice. She knew it would be tough to say good-bye to her daughter and eldest child, but Mitzie thought she was ready. She also had planned to pray with Kari before returning home and leaving her at school (hundreds of miles away). She was so prepared that she had even rehearsed her final speech. But the situation didn't work out the way she planned. Mitzie says: "I wanted to pray and give my little talk before leaving her on campus and flying home, but I was just too emotional. I realized then that I could do nothing else. I just had to trust God for her."

As the husband of a friend drove Mitzie to the airport, she cried the whole time. She recalls, "That poor man driving me around—he didn't know what to do with me."

When Gail and I took Kara to college, the three of us quickly became immersed in activity, unpacking the car, getting her settled in the dorm, and meeting her roommate and many other parents and students. Then Gail and I hustled off to our orientation process—touring the campus, hearing from the college president and deans, and talking with coaches and teachers. Those two days were packed with seminars, socials, and special events. We all had fun and seemed to be ready for this big step in Kara's life and the new challenges ahead.

Then suddenly it was over, and we had to leave. Walking away, without our "little girl," was pretty tough. And I remember wondering if we had done all we could to send her off right.

I'm sure you have the same concerns. So the question we want to answer in this chapter is simply, "What should we do the day they leave?" It's helpful to make those plans now before you get caught in the last-minute swirl of activities and emotions. Here are a few answers, the most important, of which, is the first.

GIVE YOUR BLESSING

A "blessing" is simply letting your child know that you accept and love him or her, just as he or she is, that this child is special, and that you know God has a wonderful future laid out for him or her. This concept comes from the Old Testament practice of a father blessing his children. The father would place his hands on his children and speak and pray over them, one by one. Check out Genesis 49 as an example.

Giving the blessing doesn't mean that you approve of the child's every action and choice, but that you appreciate what he or she is like on the inside: character, values, and life direction. In essence, you are saying, "You're a good kid! I'm sure glad that you are my son (or daughter). And I know you're headed in the right direction and will turn out great!"

In their classic book, *The Blessing* (Nashville, TN: Thomas Nelson Publishers, 1986), John Trent and Gary Smalley explain that blessing a child should include these five elements:

- Meaningful Touch—connecting physically (hand on the shoulder, handshake, embrace, etc.)

- Spoken Words—expressing verbally

- High Value Messages—communicating the person's being important and precious to us and to God

- Vision of a Special Future—picturing positive outcomes

- Active Commitment—working with the child to fulfill those predictions

So when we bless someone, especially a child or young person, we should involve all five elements.

Every person needs affirmation. Usually we restrict our compliments to accomplishments: good grades, excellent performance, nice game, or great job. That's fine—our kids need to be affirmed for what they do that is good, right, and noteworthy—but the blessing goes deeper. It includes affirming character qualities such as loyalty, sincerity, spirituality, integrity, faithfulness, honesty, commitment, and others. In essence, a blessing focuses on the heart of the person—what he or she is like on the inside.

Sometimes we wait until a project is finished or a goal is accomplished before commenting positively. However, we can praise progress. We know that no person is perfect—we certainly aren't.

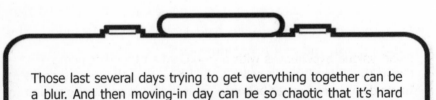

Those last several days trying to get everything together can be a blur. And then moving-in day can be so chaotic that it's hard to think about anything other than getting settled. You will be preoccupied with the nuts and bolts of moving that child out of their house and into another place. In the case of our daughter, Dana, we just barely had enough time to get her in and settled before she had to run out for a variety of appointments. So be prepared for that and set some time aside a week or two beforehand to spend some quality family time together.

Betsy Schmitt

Everyone is still in process, with ups and downs, successes and failures, and growing pains. Don't you love it when someone notices your hard effort and thanks you for it? So do your kids.

A meaningful blessing includes a statement about the future, so we have no better time than now to bless our kids, as they are looking ahead, probably with some apprehension, and stepping out on their own and away from us.

We need to be sincere and honest when we make these statements. And we should avoid flattering superlatives such as these: "You are the best in the world" or "That was the greatest example ever of..." or "Unbelievable—you are absolutely fantastic!" or "You could be the next 'American Idol.'" Think of how you feel when someone makes a similar comment to you—probably a bit embarrassed. While you appreciate the compliment, you know you aren't that good. Like the father who told his daughter, "You're the prettiest girl in the whole school!" He meant well, but his daughter was thinking, "Really? You haven't seen all the girls in my school, so how would you know?" Our blessings should be simple and sincere expressions of how we feel and what we see in our children. We

I had unique experiences with my sons when they left home. For Grant, the oldest, it was college. To be honest, there were some "male dominance" issues between us at the time, and I was feeling rather good about his leaving home and having his own territory. We packed him up, and dropped him off at the dorm with all of the typical fanfare a parent can give. Getting back in the car I gave a "whew, glad that's done" sigh of relief.

We got home about forty-five minutes later, and as we walked through the back door, I only got a few steps into the house before I realized that I needed to lock the door behind me. Then I burst out in private tears realizing that for the first time in eighteen years Grant wasn't coming home that night.

Ron DiCianni

could say, for example, "I see these qualities in you . . . " or "I really appreciate it when you . . . " or "I just had to say thank you for being such a great son!"

When we think of it that way, blessing our children, even our teenagers, will be easy. Children of all ages need their parents' blessing, but especially at this age as they are leaving home.

I'll never forget when Mom and Dad dropped me off at college. I was settled in my room, and the orientation had ended. We had said our good-byes—I had kissed Mom and had shaken Dad's hand. Then, just before Dad got into the car, he looked me in the eye, put a hand on my shoulder, and, choking back the tears, said, "Thanks for being such a good son and for being a good example for your brothers and sister." It wasn't much—just a short sentence—but it meant the world to me. Dad was giving me his blessing and telling me that as I was moving into a new era in my life, he was confident that I would do well.

Decades later, I read the following in his personal reflections: "When it became obvious to me that Ralph and Paul were following the same pattern as Dave, I made a point of telling Dave how much I appreciated the good example he had set for his brothers—and I meant every word."

Obviously, the moment meant much to my father as well.

Be sure to give your son or daughter your blessing, telling of your approval, saying how proud you are, reassuring him or her of your love, and assuring your child of your hope and confidence in the direction that his or her life is taking. You should do this in person, privately, one on one, on the day of departure. You should also reaffirm your statement on the phone and through cards and letters. Gail was terrific at this. Remembering how much college students love to get mail, she sent Kara (and then Dana) cards from time to time, all four years. Inside each card, Gail jotted a brief note expressing her joy at having such a wonderful daughter, reminding her of our love, and promising to pray for her. The girls mentioned often how much those little notes meant to them.

When each of his three children left home, Neil composed a "wallet blessing." This was a folded index card that would fit in the child's wallet or purse. It was a parting gift. Neil wrote brief words of blessing and encouragement, mentioning specific Scripture verses that had been part of that child's history. He tried to make his words of wisdom fit the character and interests of that child. Neil's first two kids, boys, left home over a decade ago. In a recent conversation with his sons, Neil mentioned the cards. To his surprise and delight, both boys pulled out their wallets and produced their copies of the aged and worn cards. One said that the original card had gotten so worn that he had made a photocopy for his wallet and was keeping the original in a safe place. Neil adds, "Sometimes blessings return upon your head."

But let's be honest. Some parents may find giving the blessing to be very difficult. Quite frankly, they struggle with their feelings for their children at this time. If the child is taking a defiant or rebellious stance, they won't want to "bless" that negative attitude. Others may find it difficult to forget the past. In both cases, blessing the child can seem contrived, phony.

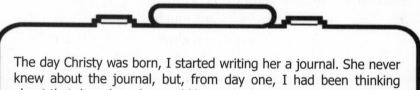

The day Christy was born, I started writing her a journal. She never knew about the journal, but, from day one, I had been thinking about that day when she would leave the house. As we were getting ready to drive home after a couple of days of freshmen orientation, I hugged her, kissed her, and handed her the journal, without any explanation. (Even as I am writing this more than four years later, I have tears running down my cheeks, and the person sitting next to me on the plane must think I am really weird.) Christy called me that night, and with both of us in tears, we expressed our love and commitment to each other.

Jim Burns

If you find yourself in a similar situation, please take a few minutes and consider all the positive, good qualities about your son or daughter. Then build on that. Don't make stuff up or make statements that both you and your child know aren't true or that you don't really believe. One dad shared the following with me: "Between us, Kyle was a pain in the posterior all through junior and senior high. We didn't seem to agree on anything and were always butting heads. So I could hardly wait till he was out of the house. But as that day came closer, I got to thinking of how I really did love him. I also felt guilty about a bunch of the stuff I had said and how I had treated him the past few years. Anyway, I took him aside one day and said that although we hadn't gotten along, I was really happy to have him as my son. I said I loved him and hoped only the best for him. Then I mumbled a bit about God and shook his hand. Actually, it was pretty awkward, and I sure was uncomfortable. But, looking back, I think it meant a lot to Kyle—not so much what I said but that I made the effort."

Giving the blessing can be a very meaningful experience for you and your child and may even be a turning point in your relationship.

Our children have done what they've done and become what they are. And they're at the threshold of their next phase of life. So we need to release, forgive, and bless.

MAKE THE DAY MEMORABLE

In addition to blessing your child, here are more suggestions for making the day memorable, in a good way. These actions, taken by parents, proved to be very positive experiences.

The mother of one student at Northwestern University and another at New York University, Betsy Schmitt advises, "Take time out from moving day to have lunch or dinner together."

She adds, "Then I suggest either writing a note sending the child off or presenting him or her with a photo album you have prepared (they will be sure to take their friends' pictures with them!).

"I also ask my children to burn a CD of their favorite songs, so that when I listen to that CD, I think of them (that's more making a good memory for me, but it works)."

Claudia and Lee Gerwin just dropped off their daughter, Abby, at Grove City College in Pennsylvania. The morning of their trip, they had a special breakfast together. Then, on the way, they had what they called, "a sleepover for the whole family." Claudia says, "We were in a hotel room in New Castle, and we laughed and laughed at Iron Chef America."

Lee also wrote Abby a letter and smuggled it into her stuff without her or Claudia knowing about it, and he labeled it to be read the day after they got her moved in. Claudia says, "Wish I'd thought of that. But then, I was wrapped up in the practical—just call me 'Martha.' My mom also baked cookies and boxed them up, and we smuggled those into her other stuff too. We also went back after we left (Abby was in a meeting) and hung a bag of dark chocolate kisses on her dorm door as a surprise when she returned to the room.

"And before we left, we prayed together."

David and Gwen Hubbard now have two children in college, Elizabeth at Vanderbilt and "Jip" at Baylor. Before Elizabeth left for school, Gwen put together an album of pictures for her with reminders of how God had blessed and been involved in her life. She selected a variety of Scripture passages that were applicable and held special meaning for Elizabeth. A friend from church helped with the layout of the book and provided his skills as a calligrapher for the verses and other text. They hoped that during times of discouragement or disappointment, this album would serve as a good reminder of God's faithfulness throughout her life.

They also held an open house/graduation party in late May for each child, which gave them the opportunity to celebrate with friends from school and church, teachers, and family friends.

At the school, after moving Jip in and just before leaving for the airport to return home, David and Gwen had a short time of prayer, blessing, and dedication in their son's dorm room. David says, "Actually, we had planned to make this longer, but we had to adjust because of the arrival of Jip's roommate and family. But still we had a very meaningful time. We needed to pray together, and I'm glad we did."

Others have made these suggestions:

- Take a long "prayer walk" together, the night before or the morning of.

- Frame a new family picture and bring it with you. Just before you leave, present it to your son or daughter.

- Establish a tradition that you follow each time you visit campus—eating at a unique restaurant, sharing a special snack, or something similar.

- Make the trip itself memorable, taking your time to get to your destination and making a couple of fun stops along the way.

- Get to the city a day early and go sightseeing.

The departure day can be traumatic, but it need not be so. Work to make it memorable and positive, giving your blessing and using your creativity.

Conversations

Although you've planned for the departure day for months and years, suddenly it will be here. It's important, therefore, to plan ahead for how you will say good-bye, for making the day meaningful for everyone.

1. When did you receive your parents' blessing? How did you feel?

2. What do you appreciate most about your son or daughter? What can you do to bless him or her?

3. How do you think he or she will respond?

4. What will you do to make departure day memorable?

5. How will prayer fit into your plan?

Letting go is a heart-attitude that begins at birth.
—Carol Kuykendall

Chapter 5

GRANTING YOURSELF PERMISSION TO GRIEVE

"You always hurt the one you love" is the plaintive refrain of a song popular decades ago. I remember hearing that as a kid and thinking, "Whatever." I couldn't appreciate the singer's lament. My immature idea of love was all sweetness and light, goose bumps and thrills—a long way from pain.

Since then, I've experienced the highs and lows of love. I have learned that the singer was right, and, further, that love always hurts.

OF LOVE AND PAIN

Most of us dislike pain and avoid it as much as possible. In fact, people who do the opposite are given a name: masochists.

Our initial experience of the connection between love and pain most likely came when we lost a loved one. Whether a romantic breakup or the death of a pet, we felt genuine grief and shed real tears. So that's probably the first example that comes to mind. But love hurts in other ways as well.

We feel pain when someone we love makes hurtful statements out of frustration or anger. We would ignore a stranger calling us names. Not so with a close relationship. What that person says carries weight, and we don't enjoy painful words.

When we love someone, truly love someone, we empathize with that person's feelings. So when he or she hurts, we hurt—we really do feel his or her pain. Remember your child screaming out and crying almost uncontrollably after taking a tumble and skinning a knee? The injury may have been minor, but the hurt was real. You felt it too.

Or how about your child's first shot in the doctor's office? Your young one looked at you with tear-filled, pleading eyes, as if to say, "How could you do this to me? How could you allow me to go through this? I thought you loved me!" But the pain was a result of your love. You knew that your child needed to be inoculated in order to protect him or her against future disease.

In the same way, discipline can also be painful to both parent and child, as you undoubtedly discovered early in your parenting

> Note to a friend from a graduate's mom: "11 days and counting till she goes."
>
> On a thank-you note to that same person from the graduate: "11 days and counting!"

experience and have been reminded through the years. When you were young, before marriage and children, you probably vowed that you would never repeat your father's phrase, "This hurts me more than it hurts you!" Then, before you could stop yourself, out it came. And you understood why Dad had uttered those infamous words and why they were true. Yet you disciplined your children for their own good, to teach them the difference between right and wrong and the truth that choices and actions have consequences.

Remember, also, that in any loving relationship, we want to be with that loved one. So we feel pain in separation. We want to be near those we love, to hold them close. When you fell head over heels for the one you eventually married, moments apart seemed eternal. And the reunions were joyous! You wanted to be together. With our children we experience the same angst. Remember the first time you hired a baby-sitter? And how about the first week at summer camp? At the time, we may have joked with other parents about the welcome break, but we missed those kids—because of love. We felt the pain of separation. Love always hurts.

Now that pain has resurfaced and seems more intense as we send them away again. But this time we know that the separation is much more permanent. We hurt, and, although our children may not admit it, so do they. But we know this is best for all concerned.

BEFORE THEY GO

No wonder we struggle with sadness at this letting go. No wonder we grieve, even before the event, as we anticipate the moment of release, watching our children leave. It's all right. It's natural and good. It's a sign of love.

The Bible states more than once that a man must "leave his father and mother" in order to establish his own marriage and home—his own life (Genesis 2:24 NKJV). Compare your experience now to what your parents must have gone through when you were eighteen or so, as you set out on your own. If you enjoyed a healthy relationship with your parents, you were able to leave home with relative ease. That is, your mom and dad didn't weigh you down with guilt and other emotional baggage or attempt to control you with emotional puppet strings. Did your mother and father feel pain at this time and grieve? Certainly. Did they show it? Probably not too much. They understood that rearing you to release you was their job, their responsibility, and that pain came with the territory. Their pain was from love and for your own good.

So here's my counsel. Through the tears, thank God for what you are feeling because you know that he is using it to help your child grow and mature into a healthy adult.

THE DAY OF DEPARTURE

One of the toughest moments comes when you have that last hug, say good-bye, and turn for home. It's a moment of truth, when reality hits. Some handle this better than others, of course. For many, the good-bye moment can be traumatic.

Neil and Sherrie Wilson's oldest son, Matt, enlisted in the air force as a high school junior, so they had a year to get used to the idea. Neil says: "It was a different kind of leaving, an unexpected form of letting go. Matt's choice was neither impulsive nor rebellious. He wasn't one of those kids who abhor discipline and join the marines to live the carefree life! But he had demonstrated to us that his skills and interests were primarily hands-on. The idea of four more years of classroom academics had little appeal, but training and working with tools and machines sounded great. The more we learned about his choice, the more we felt it fit him.

"For us, letting go had a strange finality. It wasn't like sending a son or daughter off to school, knowing that he or she could come home to us almost at will. If basic training proved to be too difficult, we would not be able to send him bus fare. We weren't setting our child free; we were letting him enter a different system of restraints, similar to a family. Also, in the back of our minds lurked the idea that we might be blessing our child to step into harm's way. Suddenly the military details in the daily news took on a new immediacy and intimacy. The flag became a symbol of cherished values.

"For our two other children, big brother's departure came with heartwarming tenderness. We all endured the lip trembling at the bus stop, but the kids wept their grief as the Greyhound pulled away. All of us sat in the car and cried together for a while. The moment was an intense mixture of love and emptiness."

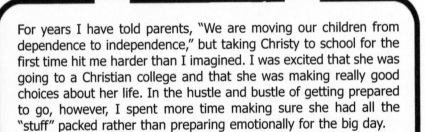

For years I have told parents, "We are moving our children from dependence to independence," but taking Christy to school for the first time hit me harder than I imagined. I was excited that she was going to a Christian college and that she was making really good choices about her life. In the hustle and bustle of getting prepared to go, however, I spent more time making sure she had all the "stuff" packed rather than preparing emotionally for the big day.

As we arrived on campus with our van totally packed, it began to hit me. After Cathy, Christy, and I walked into the freshmen orientation sign-up phase of the day, I excused myself, went into the nearest bathroom, and just started to cry. I cried for ten minutes; then it took another ten minutes to get some of the red out of my eyes so I wouldn't embarrass Christy. I hadn't told them what I was doing; but when I came back, Christy handed me some sunglasses and said, "You'll be all right, Dad. I'm only going to be an hour away!" They knew exactly what I had been doing.

Jim Burns

Whether you are choked by tears as you say good-bye or the sadness hits on the way back home, your grief is real, and it comes from love. Remember to focus on the love and not your grief. Then thank God for his sustaining love and for the great future he has in store for you and your child.

AFTER THEY'RE GONE

Don't be surprised when the grief resurfaces. It can return at some unexpected moments.

Reliving Memories

If your family has lived in the same house for several years, you will face daily reminders of the son or daughter who has just moved away: the bedroom, the favorite chair, childhood toys, pantry snacks, bookshelves, radio stations, video games, TV shows, chores, dirty clothes, and returning to your child's high school for other events. You'll certainly miss his or her familiar greeting after school. You may even miss the teenage stubbornness and arguments.

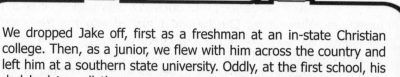

We dropped Jake off, first as a freshman at an in-state Christian college. Then, as a junior, we flew with him across the country and left him at a southern state university. Oddly, at the first school, his dad had to pull the car over to cry at the overwhelming loss of saying good-bye to our only child! But it was at the state school that I fell apart upon leaving him (my baby?) 2500 miles away from us and any other close family members. (I do think he was happy at both times to be "let go"!)

Becky Tirabassi

The garage, neighborhood, church, and school also evoke visions of your son or daughter's former life. So unless you move out of the area, you'll probably revisit and relive poignant memories daily.

My daughter Dana was very active in music during her junior high and high school years. As involved parents, Gail and I jumped in and became immersed in the music program, as choir parents, trip chaperones, and faithful attendees of every concert, competition, and musical. I remember driving Dana after her volleyball game to a friend's home in another suburb where she changed from her uniform into more suitable attire. Then we drove to the local high school where she auditioned for all-state. I prayed with her before the audition, sat near the room (and tried to hear how she was doing), and then drove her home, listening carefully to her replay every detail. Later, after she was chosen for the all-state choir, Gail and I drove downstate for the weekend activities and concert.

The year following Dana's graduation, we returned to the high school for a couple of the concerts and the spring musical. It wasn't easy because so much reminded me of those great times with Dana when I would hear her soaring soprano solos, well up with pride, and bask in the reflected glory.

Memories may include teaching your child how to ride a bike, working in the garden together, driving to Grammy and Papa's house, listening to piano recitals, helping coach the soccer team, helping a neighbor together, having family devotions, reconciling after a blow-up, putting childhood pictures and grade reports on the fridge, making cookies, eating cookies, experiencing Christmas morning, praying before bedtime, cheering at basketball games, leading him or her to Christ, taking long walks together, enjoying vacation trips, sitting in the hospital emergency room, and celebrating confirmation. The list could go on and on.

No wonder we're sad. I'm having a tough time just listing those items because they remind me of so many experiences with my little, now grown, girls.

Sensing the Loss

Another cause for sorrow at home is our profound sense of loss. As one woman described the experience, when a child leaves and moves away, you can feel as though someone has died. Actually, someone has—the child of the past: the cute and cuddly baby and toddler; the inquisitive, happy, and innocent kindergartner and elementary school child; the changing and challenging junior higher; and the rapidly growing and accomplishing senior higher. The baby, toddler, child, kid, and student are gone. In their place stands an adult, a grown-up person. We grieve that loss.

One mother explained that her daughter became an independent adult during college, especially after going on a six-month development project to a remote village in Honduras. The mom explained that she had to come to terms with the fact that her daughter didn't need her anymore, at least in the everyday activities of her life. She added, "It's nice to be needed. That's part of the loss."

At times like these, it's helpful to remember those other growing pains, how you felt at other poignant moments and how you made it through. For example, most mothers of newborns can't wait till the child can crawl and then walk and talk. Yet when that happens, they often will express some sadness over not having the "baby" anymore. That seems to occur at nearly every stage of life, especially at the loss of innocence, when the child becomes aware of evil in the world. Yet, responsible parents wouldn't really want their children to stay at that young age, stuck in immaturity.

Instead, we celebrate evidences of growth, rejoicing at moments like these:

- You notice that your son has become a "man"—tall, strong, and self-assured.

- Your junior higher suddenly begins showing interest in members of the opposite sex.

- When you're feeling down, look up—"Look up into the heavens. Who created all the stars? He brings them out one after another, calling each by its name. And he counts them to see that none are lost or have strayed away" (Isaiah 40:26).
- When you begin to regret, remember—"Great is his faithfulness; his mercies begin afresh each day" (Lamentations 3:23).
- When you fear the future, trust—"Don't be troubled. You trust God, now trust in me [Jesus]" (John 14:1).
- When you feel alone, know he's near—"And I am convinced that nothing can ever separate us from his love. Death can't, and life can't. The angels can't, and the demons can't. Our fears for today, our worries about tomorrow, and even the powers of hell can't keep God's love away. Whether we are high above the sky or in the deepest ocean, nothing in all creation will ever be able to separate us from the love of God that is revealed in Christ Jesus our Lord" (Romans 8:38–39).
- When you're unsure where to go, follow—"We do this by keeping our eyes on Jesus, on whom our faith depends from start to finish" (Hebrews 12:2).

- Your daughter demonstrates wisdom beyond her years as she makes a responsible choice.

- Your child begins to ask tough questions about the world and theology.

- Your older child provides a good model for the younger siblings.

So focus on the positive, on the growth and maturity and independence of your former "baby," "kid," and "young teen." God has begun his good work and will continue it (Philippians 1:6).

SHARING YOUR FEELINGS

Here's a final word on your sadness: be honest with your feelings without driving everyone crazy. In other words, don't worry about letting people know how you feel, especially when they ask. Even then, however, be sure to balance the negative with the positive. You can say, for example, "Quite honestly, I'm struggling because I really miss [your child]. Some days are better than others. But I know that [he or she] is in the right place. It's amazing how quickly our kids grow up! And I have to add that my tears are also mixed with joy—I'm so proud of my [son or daughter]!"

What you don't want is for people to think, "Oh no—here [he or she] comes again with another tale of woe!" and then avoid you. The idea is to be honest and realistic. And your God-honoring, positive attitude can be a real encouragement to others who are facing similar challenges.

CONVERSATIONS

Bearing and rearing children brings countless moments of joy. But parenting also involves difficult struggles, pain, and grief. That's part of what it means to be an imperfect human being living in an imperfect world.

1. When did you first become aware that love could bring pain?

2. Why is change painful? In what ways has this current change in your family been painful to you? To your child? What evidence of growth do you already see in your child as a result of this change?

3. How have the events of the past several months strengthened your endurance? Your character? In what ways has your faith matured?

4. When did you begin to grieve your child's departure? How did you respond to those feelings?

5. Which of God's promises gives you the most hope during this time?

6. What signs of maturity in your son or daughter cause you the most joy?

*Mom always liked
you better!*
—Tom Smothers

Chapter 6

ANTICIPATING CHANGES TO THE FAMILY STRUCTURE

After a family member leaves, the first obvious change is the structure of the family itself. We parents should anticipate this, but often we don't.

THE EFFECTS OF BIRTH ORDER

When the oldest child, or the next one in line, leaves home, everyone moves up in the pecking order. Whether or not this actually happens, children think it does. The new "oldest" child often assumes responsibility and feels empowered. Mom and Dad will probably also make new chore assignments for the remaining siblings. This change affects everyone at home.

Being the oldest child can be a pain (asserted confidently by one—an oldest child, that is, not a pain). This child is the "trailblazer"; every one of his or her initial childhood experiences is the first for Mom and Dad as well. In addition, many parents are overprotective of their firstborn "little darling," worried about every whimper and low-grade fever. And although they would never admit to doing this, most of these fledgling moms and dads experiment with the firstborn, trying various approaches to feeding, playing, disciplining, and educating.

Then, as this child gets older, he or she often has to assume a number of responsibilities around the house—for example, cleaning, mowing, shoveling, and baby-sitting—while the other siblings have lighter chores. Ask any firstborn about what it means to live in that position, and you'll probably hear something like, "It wasn't easy," followed by a litany of personal examples.

But being the first also comes with certain perks. For example, the eldest child tends to be in all the picture albums and have the most toys. And, if other children follow, this son or daughter is the only one to have been an "only child" for a while.

I'm the firstborn of five siblings. One of my perks was having a room of my own for as far back as I can remember, while my next two siblings, brothers Ralph and Paul, had to share a bedroom.

Also, as the first to drive, I often could use the family car for dates and other activities. Sure I had to act as chauffeur, but I was in control when I drove, and I liked it.

As the trailblazer, the oldest child is usually the first one to leave home, so it will be a new experience for all concerned: the child, the parents, and the rest of the family. As with other significant life events, everyone involved has a better idea of what to expect if they've already experienced something similar. Thus, in some families, the departure of the firstborn can be traumatic.

In a family where the last remaining child (or an only child) is leaving home, the change may be even more dramatic for the parents, as they begin to experience the "empty nest."

When the Oldest Child in a Large Family Leaves

Whether this is an only daughter with three younger brothers, a son with numerous younger siblings of both sexes, or the first child in a family with three children, the families have at least this in common: everyone in the family is charting new territory. This

Just like we eventually have to let go when we are training our children to ride bikes, we need to give them a shove and let them go as they grow to adulthood. We do not have an alternative. Can you imagine a parent running alongside her son's bicycle, steadying him as he rides to middle school? Sometimes our support means letting go.

Letting go communicates to our teens that we believe in them. We are saying, "I've provided connection, direction, and motivation. Now I'm letting you go because you can take it from here." But letting go isn't always easy—particularly for the parent.

Timothy Smith, *The Seven Cries of Today's Teens* (Brentwood, TN: Integrity Publishers, 2003), 207.

eldest child is the first to leave, so the experience is brand-new for the rest of the kids, as well as for Mom and Dad.

Through the last decade plus, the older sibling has received much attention, either negatively for mistakes and poor choices or positively for achievements and awards. And those who follow must deal with his or her reputation.

How this plays out depends on many factors that we don't have time and space to discuss here: the type of behavior and degree of success of the older one; the differences in sex, physical size, and abilities of the siblings; the number of years between kids; the mobility of the family; and so forth. But in virtually all of these situations, the younger children stand in the shadow, for better or worse, of the older ones.

It's not easy to follow someone with a strong reputation. And for many years, the younger kids have heard teachers and others make statements like these:

- "So you're Sally's sister. I can see the resemblance. You must be a math whiz too!"

- "Uh oh, another Thompson kid. Get out the detention pad."

- "I'm really disappointed in your performance. Your brother was such a good student; I'm surprised."

You may already be aware of the problem in your family, having had to deal with it in the earlier grades. But this issue usually comes to a head during the adolescent years. Some teens just want to shout, "I'm not my [brother or sister]. I'm me!"

Each person wants to be accepted for who he or she is, to blaze a new trail in life, to establish his or her own reputation. Sometimes we see this playing out in the classes and extracurricular activities they choose.

Many years ago, a sophomore student named Mike became very

involved in my Campus Life ministry. Mike had two younger brothers, Chris and Tom. The brothers were a couple of years apart, so when Mike was a junior, Chris was a freshman. Although Mike attended every meeting and went on every trip, I couldn't get Chris interested in the program, even when we had a Campus Life club meeting at his house. As soon as Mike graduated, however, Chris got involved

> We've all seen a version of those advertisements for home equity loans. The boy calls home from school, straining to be heard and to hear in the chaos of the dorm hallway. Mom listens intently and smiles. Then her son says, "So, Mom, I was thinking about a quick trip home this weekend . . . "
>
> The camera switches back to Mom and zooms back to display Mom and Dad relaxing in a hot tub in a beautifully decorated master bath. She covers the phone before she says to her husband, "Junior wants to come home this weekend. Shall we break the news about what we did with his room?"

and was active for his final two years of high school. But, then, Tom followed the same pattern and didn't come until Chris had graduated. It was as though the younger boys didn't want to encroach on the older one's turf.

Sometimes the next child after a high-achieving sibling will seem to lose interest in school altogether, adopting a nonchalant, apathetic attitude. It's as though he or she is saying, "Why compete? I'll never be as good or do as well. And who cares? I certainly don't." Some may choose alternate classes and activities in which to excel. I know a family where the older daughter was outstanding at volleyball, achieving all-conference and honorable mention all-state awards. Her sister, four years younger and probably a better athlete, showed no interest in volleyball and even made fun of the sport to her friends. Instead, she played some basketball and then dropped sports altogether to concentrate on music. The statement couldn't have been clearer: "I'm not my sister. I'm me!"

Others have responded by attending a different college than the older brother or sister, insisting on going to a different church or youth ministry, dressing weird and acting indifferent or rebellious, or something similar. Most of these kids don't understand what motivates or pushes them in the new direction. They just act.

The best action you can take is to spend time with the child who is next in line. Just do stuff together. Consider it an investment. On one of those occasions, have a heart-to-heart talk with this child. Again, I recommend that you do this away from the house; you could go out to breakfast, for example. In any case, explain to your son or daughter that you appreciate what makes him or her unique and that you don't expect him or her to be like the older child, the one who has just left home. In fact, you are thrilled that God has designed and gifted each child the way he has. Jump right in and ask about those times when the younger one has felt the burden of the older and when he or she has thought that you have had those expectations. Ask for help in letting you know when you seem to be doing that.

You may need to have this discussion more than once. It's similar to giving the blessing (discussed in chapter 4).

Some kids have no problem with following an older sibling through life. They may even see it as a motivating factor. But bring up the topic anyway. Your child needs to know that you want the best for him or her and that you appreciate how special he or she is. Again, affirm this child and pronounce him or her as "good" and "much loved."

We don't want our other children to feel overlooked or forgotten, floundering in the wake of the older ones who are speeding off in life. This problem is prevalent in medium and large families.

When the Next-to-Last Child Leaves

When the next-to-last child leaves, only one child is left at home. Certainly the child left behind may have to deal with the issue we just discussed. But another one surfaces with the final child in this family structure. (Note: this also applies to an only child.) This child, the baby in the family, becomes the object of

> Note from a graduating guy to a good friend of his mother: "Take care of my mom because I'm the last one to go."

all the parental attention and, often, the burden of many of the parents' dreams, especially if the older kids have been "average" or worse.

This isn't limited to the parents; many times the older siblings lay the burden on the child. As I mentioned before, I'm the oldest of five siblings. I have one sister and three brothers. Like me, my brothers Ralph and Paul were into sports in high school and college, especially football. So as soon as we could, we dressed little Philip in pads and taught him how to pass, catch, block, and tackle. (I think I placed a football in his crib.) And I remember our standing along the sidelines and cheering for him in junior tackle league games. Looking back, I can see that we were trying to fulfill our dreams through him. Phil almost *had* to be a football player—we gave him no choice.

Or perhaps you've seen a little girl dressed like a contestant in a beauty pageant. Someone in the family wanted her to grow up too soon. And I've known parents to push their early adolescents socially, encouraging kids as young as fifth or sixth grade to date.

In addition to sports, appearance, and relationships, the youngest child may have to deal with unrealistic expectations in the mental or spiritual areas of life as well.

We parents need to fight this temptation for all we're worth. No child should have to bear the pressure of fulfilling the parents' dreams, of making them happy. We may have experienced dream adjustment with an older child (see chapter 3), but we shouldn't then place that expectation on a younger one. We need to help *all* our children, from oldest to youngest, discover their unique temperaments, talents, gifts, and interests, and help them make *their own* way in life.

Here's another challenge for the parents and their last child. Sometimes Mom and Dad think they're ready for this stage in their lives because they've had a long time to prepare and have, successfully, launched several older brothers and sisters. That's true, to a certain extent, because these parents have had practice at saying good-bye and making the family adjustments. But coming to the end of the line can be a rude awakening, especially for couples whose lives, for virtually all of their marriage, have revolved around the children. Suddenly they realize that not only will their family never be the same but also that they are coming to the end of an era. So don't view your last child as your last opportunity to fulfill your dreams for your children.

Older brothers and sisters will often claim that the baby of the family has been raised differently and, in some cases, spoiled. Sometimes that happens because of the number of years that stand between the first child and the last. In my case, for example, as the oldest child, I had the advantage of having youthful parents. I can remember watching my father play on the church softball team and having him participate in sports with me—playing catch, hitting groundballs and fly balls, and shooting baskets. My brother Phil, thirteen years my junior, has no such memories. Dad had long since given up playing sports and probably was too worn out when he came home from work to do much participating. Also, I can remember when we got our first car and our first television set (now that dates me!). As a young teen, Phil had his own TV.

In addition, parenting styles tend to change through the years. Take discipline, for example. I'm sure that I received much more severe penalties than any of my siblings (they may dispute that, but I'm pretty sure it's true). By the time Phil came around, Mom and Dad either were too tired to be real strict or had mellowed. (Or perhaps Phil was just better behaved? Nah!) And when Phil was the last child at home, Mom and Dad had no other kids to divide their attention; he received it all (for better or worse).

My point is simply that the youngest child holds a special place, and his or her parents may find it even more difficult than they suspected to release this child. So when the next-to-last child has left, Mom and Dad begin to imagine, negatively, what life will be like when all the kids are gone. And they may place this burden on the remaining youngster. Whether or not a parent says this, the child often hears, "What will I do when you're gone? The house will be so empty. I wish you didn't have to grow up!"

Be sensitive to those feelings in yourself. And be very careful of investing all of yourself in this child. Seize the opportunity of spending quality time with your son or daughter. But allow him or her to grow up and move out like the others—to sprout wings and fly away.

When the First of Two Children Leaves

At this point you may ask, "Wait a minute. What's so special about this family configuration?" Good question. Certainly the younger child in this type of family may face the issues and challenges that we just covered: following in the footsteps of an older sibling and being the baby of the family. (So be sure to follow the guidelines I've outlined above.) But I have included the two-child family as a separate category because in this family, everyone gets a double-whammy, all at once. Just after Mom and Dad have their first experience of letting go, they return home to an "only child," the last one before their "empty nest."

If you are in this situation, you know what I'm talking about—you know the feelings. Instead of focusing on the negative, however, these parents should see the positive, the opportunities that now present themselves. Here are a few.

In most two-children families, the kids are usually a few years apart in age. So that gives the parents some time to prepare for the next release. They can learn from the first experience and apply it to the second. For example, having just done this a year or so ago, they know how to schedule the college visits and the application process. They also know how to pack for college, what to expect during orientation, and what to ask of university staff and faculty. And because the kids are fairly close in age, they can suggest a visit by the younger to the older during the school year and then work to make it happen.

If this is your family configuration, remember that you can now spend more time with the younger child and deepen your relationship with him or her. You can also work at preparing your heart and your child's for the very soon occasion of his or her leaving home.

During my years in youth ministry, I had often advised parents to take their children to breakfast, one on one, and had said that this would be a great way to enhance communication and build the relationship with a son or daughter. But as my own daughter, Dana, approached her senior year in high school, I realized that I hadn't done that with my girls, and time was running out. So, feeling a bit guilty, the week before school was to begin, I asked Dana if she would like to go to breakfast with me the first day of classes. She answered matter-of-factly, "Sure."

That Thursday, we got up early (very early for me); school began at 7:15 and was twenty minutes from our house, and we had to have time to eat and talk . . . you get the idea. Anyway, we got to the restaurant, had breakfast together, and had a great time of talking about all sorts of issues, mostly related to the beginning of the school year, her senior year. Afterward, I dropped off Dana at school and then drove to work, a bit sleepy but feeling good about myself as a dad. I thought, "That was nice," but quickly put it out of my mind.

The next week rolled around, and Dana said, "Are we going to breakfast this week?" And I discovered that *she* had enjoyed the time too. So every Thursday morning of Dana's senior year we ate together and talked and laughed and prayed. Sometimes the conversations were light and superficial. But every now and then we got deeper and had real breakthroughs.

OPPORTUNITIES

Check out these stories of God-given opportunities:

- Exodus 11:9—When Pharaoh would not listen to God even after the ten plagues, it gave God opportunity to do more mighty miracles in Egypt.
- Judges 14:4—Samson's parents didn't realize when Samson wanted to marry a Philistine woman that God was creating an opportunity to disrupt the Philistines.
- 1 Samuel 24:4—David had the opportunity to kill Saul but spared his life.
- Proverbs 10:5—A wise youth works hard; a shameful youth sleeps away opportunity.
- Jeremiah 46:17—Egypt missed an opportunity to conquer Babylon.
- Zephaniah 2:2—The prophet gave God's call for Judah to repent before the opportunity was blown away like chaff.
- Matthew 10:18; Mark 13:9; Luke 21:13—Jesus told the apostles that when they were arrested, it would be their opportunity to tell governors and kings about him.
- Luke 19:44—Jesus wept over Jerusalem who rejected God's opportunity for peace.
- John 11:15—Because Jesus went to Lazarus after Lazarus had died, the apostles had another opportunity to believe.
- Acts 3:12—After John and Peter healed the crippled beggar, Peter capitalized on the opportunity to teach the people about Jesus.
- Acts 5:31—The apostles taught their arresting Jewish leaders that Jesus' resurrection gives the people of Israel the opportunity to repent.

> - Galatians 6:10—When we have opportunity we should do good to everyone, especially Christians.
> - Ephesians 5:16—Make the most of every opportunity for doing good.
> - Colossians 4:5—Live wisely among non-Christians, and make the most of every opportunity.
> - James 1:2—Let trouble be an opportunity for joy.
> - Revelation 13:10—Even though people around you are being persecuted, it is your opportunity to have endurance and faith.

At times like those you can cover everything from friends to future, from relationships to religion, from theater to theology. And who knows, you may even learn something!

Use the time after the release of your first son or daughter to build and prepare for the second. Take the opportunities God gives you to invest in your kids.

SIBLING REACTIONS

Right after I left for college, Ralph moved into what had been my room and became "the oldest," with all the rights and privileges of that "exalted" position. I'm not sure what all of those were, except for the room and the use of the family car after he got his license, but he felt as though he had moved up in his life station.

Although we had our typical sibling battles, Ralph and I have always been very close. In fact, when I went off to college, I could tell that he was very proud of me and almost idolized me. I remember getting letters from Ralph, at football camp and during the first couple of months of school. When I went home at Thanksgiving, however, I sensed a tension between us, as though he resented me being there. Then I realized what was happening. With my vacancy, Ralph was now the oldest child at home, the senior member of the troop, and clearly enjoying that position. I returned, expecting things to be as they had been, but the family dynamic had changed. Ralph was fifteen and beginning to make a name for himself in high school. He was asserting himself in the family and receiving a lot of attention from Mom and Dad. When I returned, I was a threat to his new role. I quickly realized that I had to back off and act more like a guest than big brother. Things had changed.

I would have been more prepared for Ralph's reactions if my parents had said something like this: "Dave, we really want you to know how much we appreciate you and what a fine big brother you have been. We can see how much your brothers and sister look up to you and love you. And we're all very excited about this next phase of your life and what God has in store for you.

"We want to bring up one issue, however, that we haven't mentioned before. It's not a big deal, but we want to prepare you so you won't be surprised.

"When you leave, our family at home will be different. Instead of seven of us around the dinner table, we'll have six. And because you won't be here, we won't enjoy your jokes or be able to talk about everything you did during the day. That will leave a hole, but we're pretty sure it will be filled, especially by Ralph and Paul.

"Speaking of changes, Ralph and Paul will have them too. Up till now, they've shared a bedroom. But we're giving Ralph your bedroom so that he and Paul can each have a room of their own. Ralph, now as the oldest child at home, will have some of the privileges you enjoyed. He'll also get some of your old chores (he doesn't know that yet).

"We say all this because we don't want you to assume that when you come home everything will return to the way it was. You will be changing, and so will our family. You are growing up, maturing; so are your brothers and sister. These changes are good, but they may be confusing at times while everyone adjusts.

"We love you, will miss you terribly, and will long for your return. But you'll see and sense the changes, and we just wanted you to know that they're coming and to be prepared. If you ever wonder what's going on, why we seem to be treating you differently at Thanksgiving, Christmas, spring break, or summer, remember this conversation. It'll be fine."

You probably should have a similar talk, and then a family meeting, with the rest of the family, after the older son or daughter has left, to help everyone understand and anticipate what will happen. During this meeting, you could explain, in general, some of the changes that your recent graduate will be experiencing away from home and on his or her own—physically, mentally, spiritually, emotionally, and so forth—and encourage every family member to celebrate those changes. Spend time praying for this older child too.

In some families the changes are obvious—everything is out there. Junior returns and demands to have his room back. Amanda begins bad-mouthing her older sister, even before she leaves. With his older brother gone, Chad is suddenly an only child at home and isn't sure how to act.

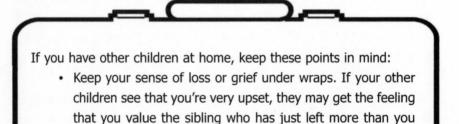

If you have other children at home, keep these points in mind:
- Keep your sense of loss or grief under wraps. If your other children see that you're very upset, they may get the feeling that you value the sibling who has just left more than you do them.
- Don't try to turn one of the remaining siblings into a mirror image of the one who has left. Both children will resent it.

Minnesota Higher Education Services Offices (www.mheso.state.mn.us)

In many families, however, the changes are subtle. No one is aware of any issues, and everything seems fine. Then a conflict or outburst may surprise you and the rest of the family, especially the graduate. That certainly was my experience. Away at college and far from the presence of my siblings, I was blissfully unaware of any problems . . . until that fateful Thanksgiving vacation. Suddenly I found myself at the center of a few storms and didn't know why.

The left-behind siblings may also resent the attention given to the returning brother or sister. Suddenly, all the questions are about the older child's activities, classes, and accomplishments during the past several months. (This is heightened when a prodigal returns.) Pushed to the sidelines, the younger kids may act out to move the spotlight back to them.

Note: this can begin *before* the child leaves home.

PRACTICAL ISSUES FOR THE NEW FAMILY STRUCTURE

The interpersonal dynamic is altered in every type of family. Maybe you can find your family in these descriptions. In each one, consider the potential changes, especially for those left at home, as the child leaves:

- The only daughter of a single mom

- The middle child in a large family but the first to move out

- The second child in a family of five (two parents and three kids), only a year younger than the oldest and following in her footsteps

- A child in a blended family

- An oldest child who has been homeschooled

- A twin

Changes in the family structure will take some getting used to, so be prepared.

After our daughter Kara left for school, our family at home was reduced by 25 percent—a big chunk. During our dinners, Kara had always been animated, as she would recount the day's activities. Sitting at one end of the table and Dana at the other, with Gail and me across from each other in the middle, Kara had been the center of attention. At times, Dana had found it difficult to break into the conversation. Then suddenly, with Kara gone, the spotlight turned and shone on Dana's end of the table. Dana noticed that Gail and I even turned our chairs somewhat in her direction. Definite change.

Brian Bobbitt says that when his daughter left for college, his son, Brock, was a bit unnerved by all the attention. He even suggested that Mom and Dad "need to have another kid."

Usually the leaving child is totally unaware of the change in family dynamics. Consumed by the new life at school, on the job, or in the military, he or she usually assumes that everything is pretty much the same back home. Even when the graduate is aware of personal changes, he or she doesn't realize that younger siblings are growing as well and that the family structure has been altered.

This can lead to reentry shock when the young person returns home and rejoins the family, even for a short period of time. Conflict, misunderstanding, and resentment can become the order of the day.

To handle these changes, the first step is to understand that they are coming. So by reading this chapter (and believing me), you are well on your way. At least the changes shouldn't surprise you.

Right now you need to be proactive. Schedule a time with your graduating son or daughter—child and parent(s) only. To make this memorable, have a special dinner at a restaurant of your child's choice. (You can also use this as the opportunity to give your blessing, as we discussed in chapter 4.) During the meal, bring up the topic casually and positively. You could mention that you've read how families change and that you've heard stories of how some families have reacted to those differences. Then you could offer suggestions for future actions and reactions.

When our older daughter, Allison, left home, the change in family dynamics was almost immediate and positive. After the first couple of weeks at school, the reticent high school senior was now eager to tell us about all her new experiences. Over her four years in college our relationship has changed from parent-child to parent-young adult. It's been wonderful, and I look forward to a deeper relationship as she enters the "real world."

Allison and her younger sister, Dana, are extremely different in temperament and interest, and during high school had very little to do with each other. We were happy to see that they became closer once Allison left. I think Dana felt the freedom to be her own person and not live in the shadow of her older sister. Interestingly enough, that relationship changed back when Dana was in her senior year and going through the college process. She withdrew from Allison as she again felt she was competing and trying to do "as well" as her older sister. Now that Dana has left for her own college experience, I'm beginning to see signs that their closer relationship is redeveloping. I'm also optimistic that Dana will once again open up to us now that she is on her own.

While we miss having the girls around, it has been more relaxed at home without the tension of two extra drivers in the house, two extra schedules and demands, and two extra people fighting for the same bathroom space, TV, and computer time. I think Kevin, the youngest, is enjoying being "the one."

Betsy Schmitt

Making New Assignments

One of the first adjustments will be to family routines and chore assignments because the family will have one less member of the team. If your older daughter, for example, has helped chauffeur younger siblings to various activities, you will have to adjust the schedule. If your graduated son had baby-sitting and lawn care responsibilities, those will have to be covered by someone else.

The best approach for making these assignments is to have a family meeting after the dust has settled following the departure of the older child. When you meet, don't just list your graduate's former chores and reassign them; instead, begin by listing all of the important tasks and responsibilities that need to be covered and suggest that all of them are up for grabs. All family members, every child, should feel part of the team, knowing that he or she can make significant contributions to the welfare of the family. You probably should discuss allowances at this time as well. I believe strongly that every family member should have jobs to do simply because he or she is part of the family. And each child should be given an allowance, financial resources, for the same reason. So this family meeting should not include a debate over whether or not a child will help with housework. No, the discussion should center on who will do what.

Keep the meeting positive and upbeat. Everyone should feel that this new era provides new opportunities.

Celebrating Individual Uniquenesses

God has created each person as a unique individual—no two people are alike. We know this, of course, but we often forget it when dealing with our children. In fact, as the younger children mature and move into the family roles and responsibilities vacated by the older sibling, Mom and Dad sometimes expect them to be and behave just like the older one.

Recently a father called to ask my counsel. Over an early break-fast he explained that he just couldn't understand his junior-high-age son (the middle child in a family of five). The oldest child, a daughter, had done just fine and was in college. The next child, the oldest son, was outgoing and interested in friends, sports, and music and was doing well in high school. The father had those same inter-ests, so he and the older kids had much in common and much to talk about. But this younger son, the thirteen-year-old, seemed shy and had chosen activities that his older siblings had ignored. He was more introverted, focusing on just a few friends. And instead of sports and music, like his older sister and brother, he was into art and computers. Dad wondered what was wrong with his boy and what he should do. He wanted his son to get out more, to be more social and athletic. I assured my friend that his younger son was fine. The boy's personality and interests were just different than his older brother's.

I know that seems obvious, and you may be thinking, "How silly—I'd never make that mistake!" Don't be too sure. These atti-tudes and expectations can creep in, unannounced and unseen. Be careful.

This is where opportunity knocks. With the older brother or sister gone, you have a great chance to deepen your relationship with your next son or daughter.

Forging Stronger Relationships

Perhaps the greatest opportunity provided by this change in the family's life is to forge new and stronger relationships with our children—those who are leaving and those still at home.

Think of the time, energy, and emotion that you have invested in your older son or daughter during the past couple of years. You may even have intensified your efforts to connect with him or her during the past few months. Hopefully, your relationship with the older child has deepened considerably, and you will continue to build on that foundation. But after that child has left, you now have many of those resources to invest in the other kids.

Some parents feel rudely awakened by the reality that their child will be leaving, and, as we have discussed, they may reflect with regret over the time wasted and opportunities missed with that older child. Regardless of what you did or didn't do in the past, see this event as a wake-up call for the present, a motivation to tend to the kids still at home. That is, don't repeat those past mistakes. Begin now to build relationships with those younger siblings.

Know this for sure: your family structure will change when the child leaves home. So be ready for the changes and use them as opportunities for deepening and building.

CONVERSATIONS

Throw a rock in a still pond and watch what happens. After the initial splash, a widening circle of ripples moves out from the center and toward the shore. A child leaving home is like the rock, and everyone sees and hears the splash. But the family also must deal with the ripples—much more subtle effects.

1. In what ways will your family structure be altered? What changes do you anticipate?

2. What can you do to minimize the negative effects of those changes?

3. What jobs and responsibilities will have to be reassigned? What's your plan for making that a fun process?

4. In what ways are your remaining children similar to your graduate in personality, temperament, gifts, interests, and talents? How are they different?

5. What's your strategy for deepening your relationship with those still at home?

I have never let my schooling interfere with my education.
—Mark Twain

Chapter 7

MOVING YOUR RELATIONSHIP TO PARENT/PEER

During this time, a poignant change occurs in the relationship we enjoy with a son or a daughter. We have seen the change coming, but now it's almost here—the boy or girl isn't a child anymore; he or she is a young adult. Thus, the relationship is in the process of changing from strictly parent to child to peer to peer.

At least that's the way it's supposed to be, right? I mean, we want our kids to grow up and become fully functioning, mature adults, able to live without us, on their own. But these next few years of transition can be a bit bumpy. In defending her "right" to make a decision, for example, a daughter might remind her mother, "After all, I *am* nineteen!" Yet this same daughter, a few days later, might call and ask for help; and the mom will be tempted to reply (with sarcasm, I must add), "You take care of it. After all, you *are* nineteen!"

Think back to when you were first on your own and growing independent from home. How did your relationship with your parents change? How did you want it to change? Some adults bemoan the fact that their parents still treat them like small children, trying to influence their decisions and control their lives. At times they feel like yelling, "I'm an adult—I'm forty, for goodness sake. I know what I'm doing!" You may feel that way every now and then; perhaps, for example, when you visit your folks at Thanksgiving or Christmas.

So the challenge is for us to make a better transition—better for us and better for our kids.

Because your child is maturing and quickly becoming an adult, you now have an excellent chance to move intentionally toward a peer relationship with him or her. We've discussed this previously. You will always be your child's parent, but you can also be a friend.

SHARING MEANINGFUL MOMENTS

One way to treat your child like an adult friend is to share significant experiences—learning together. That's what friends do. And when they have an exciting and meaningful moment or event together, their relationship bond is strengthened. So look for opportunities to participate in an activity that will give you something to talk about and bring you closer. For example, the two of you could rent and watch a thought-provoking video. You could attend a political rally or a public lecture. You could read the same book (or one person could read the book first and then pass it on to the other). You could minister side by side on a mission trip.

These activities don't have to be serious, of course. You could work out, play golf, fish, or go to a sporting event. The idea is to choose something that will enhance communication and deepen your relationship. It should be an activity that you can talk during and about. The goal should be to experience life together.

Dana and I both run to stay in shape. Although I've never seen myself as a runner, over the years I have put in plenty of miles and have finished a few marathons. One day I told my girls, "I'll run one more marathon if either of you wants to run with me." Dana took me up on it, and we trained for and then ran the Chicago Marathon a few years ago. The experience drew us closer, and it certainly became a conversation topic between us.

About six months into his life in the military, during an otherwise mundane phone conversation, my son floored me with the simple question, "So how are you doing, Dad?" The hint of peer-caring caught me by surprise. Matt was beginning to see that his father was someone who might not be doing all right and probably ought to be asked once in a while to make sure. What I tried to do was thank him for asking. I didn't know what else to say. But when I hung up the phone, I wept. We really don't understand how deep our need to be cared for by our children runs until they reveal it by caring. We never stop needing each other. The opportunities to express our need and meet each other's needs may change throughout life, but the needs will always be there.

Neil Wilson

COMMUNICATING WITH YOUR YOUNG ADULT

Another way to treat your maturing child like a friend is to ask for his or her opinion on important matters. Actually, this should begin before your child leaves home.

Years ago, a friend told me, "I will learn from you if I think you can learn from me." His point was that communication between peers and friends should be two-way. In friendship, one person doesn't dominate the conversation, speak down to the other, and have all the answers. Friends treat each other as equals, assuming that the other person has something significant to contribute.

Talk Things Over

So brainstorm and think of how you might be able to get your son or daughter involved in your life. Get creative. What questions

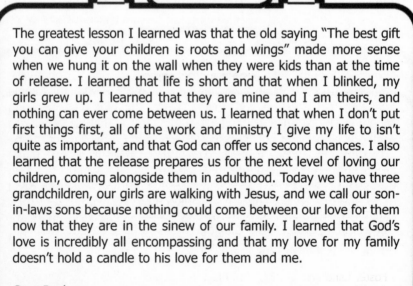

The greatest lesson I learned was that the old saying "The best gift you can give your children is roots and wings" made more sense when we hung it on the wall when they were kids than at the time of release. I learned that life is short and that when I blinked, my girls grew up. I learned that they are mine and I am theirs, and nothing can ever come between us. I learned that when I don't put first things first, all of the work and ministry I give my life to isn't quite as important, and that God can offer us second chances. I also learned that the release prepares us for the next level of loving our children, coming alongside them in adulthood. Today we have three grandchildren, our girls are walking with Jesus, and we call our son-in-laws sons because nothing could come between our love for them now that they are in the sinew of our family. I learned that God's love is incredibly all encompassing and that my love for my family doesn't hold a candle to his love for them and me.

Gary Rosberg

could you ask? What problems could you pose? Don't make up one that is superficial or silly; ask a legitimate question for which you need an answer. These issues should be age appropriate. In other words, be careful not to suddenly place a huge burden on your child's shoulders. For example, at this point don't have a heart-to-heart discussion about your current struggle with lust or about your worries over your shaky investment portfolio.

Instead, begin with something important but relatively safe and emotionally neutral. You could ask about various options for the next family vacation. You could describe a situation at church and ask for ideas on what to do. Or you could get your child's views on a political issue. And when your son or daughter responds, listen carefully and take his or her answer seriously. Don't allow conversations to be dominated by logistics, "to do" lists, and schedules. Talk about views, thoughts, and dreams.

One father told me that he called a family meeting and shared his "Last Will and Testament" with his kids, now that the oldest child was leaving. At first the kids joked about how they would divvy up certain prized family possessions. But then my friend was able to seriously discuss this very important aspect of their lives.

Parenting achieves its major goal when teens leave home and go out into the world able to cope with it and make productive contributions. . . .

Over time, your children will love and respect you more and more for teaching them how to think and how to live. As their maturity catches up to yours, you will discover that you can meet on common ground as adults, and that you have become friends. This is the greatest reward any parent can hope for.

Foster Cline and Jim Fay, *Parenting Teens with Love & Logic* (Colorado Springs, CO: Piñon Press, 1992), 152–53.

Also, in anticipation of your child's return, work at crafting thoughtful questions that you can ask about his or her life away from home. Don't ask questions that can be answered with yes, no, or another one-word response. For example, instead of asking, "Do you like your classes?" or "Have you made new friends?" (both yes or no questions) or "How was school?" or "How's the job going?" (both quick-answer questions), you could ask, "What have you been discussing in your sociology class lately?" or "What evidence do you see at work that the economy is improving?" or "How are your friends dealing with the changes at school?" Thoughtful questions treat your son or daughter as an adult and aren't perceived as intrusive.

Get into the habit of talking things over with your nearly adult son or daughter. He or she doesn't have to be home for these discussions; you can make a phone call or write a letter. Invite your child into your life.

Try Not to Argue

In becoming an adult, late adolescents are discovering their brains—trying to think like adults and to make up their own minds about important issues. In other words, they will argue. And in forming their own opinions, they often will take stands directly opposite to those held dear by their parents. Those philosophical, political, and theological disputes may threaten the relationship. It's hard to be friends with someone who seems to question everything you believe in and stand for.

For many years, we had this sign hanging in our basement: "Attention Teenagers: Leave home now, while you still know everything!"—written, no doubt, by a parent who had tired of debating with a dogmatic adolescent. I think it was Socrates who said, "The more you know, the more you realize how little you know."

Young college students haven't had enough education to realize, yet, that they don't know very much. Yet they often speak as though they do, in fact, know everything. And this can be maddening for parents.

This new freedom experienced by our released children encompasses the intellect. These graduates, especially those in college, will be exposed to new ideas and will be challenged by teachers and classmates. They will become free thinkers as they learn to think analytically and move into a phase of questioning and doubting just about everything. Someone has said (probably a parent) that the most dangerous person in the world is a college student who has taken one course in philosophy or psychology. After being exposed to either of those disciplines, students often think they have all the answers (or at least most of them). This usually leads to some interesting debates with Mom or Dad about politics or religion.

Although some of their strong statements may tempt us toward strong responses, we'll be much better off if we hold our tongues. And instead of thinking of sarcastic retorts, we should thank God that our children are developing intellectually (and pray they get through this awkward stage soon).

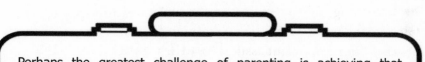

Perhaps the greatest challenge of parenting is achieving that delicate balance between letting our children go in age-appropriate ways and yet providing the undergirding for their explorations. We must resist the urge to hold them too tightly and yet always be there in the background waving at them with support and love, ready to come to their aid when they need us, protecting them from dangers they are not quite ready to handle. And somewhere along the way, as we negotiate the transition of letting them go into adulthood, we become more than parent and child. We become friends. And that is the greatest joy of all.

Adapted from Ruth Haley Barton, *The Truths That Free Us* (Colorado Springs, CO: Shaw Publishing, 2002), 169–70.

RESPONDING SO THEY'LL KEEP TALKING

Your son or daughter will soon acquire new interests, discover new information, and grapple with new ideas. In the process, he or she will be learning how to think critically, how to evaluate, and how to express his or her opinions.

Remember your child's first words? The little one exclaimed, "Mama," "Papa," "No!" or "Uh oh," and you were thrilled. As the child grew, he or she increased in vocabulary and in communication skills. At times you wished your child wouldn't talk so much. Then, during junior high and high school, you had to peer behind the one-word answers and try to pry out more conversation.

In the next few years, your son or daughter will gain knowledge, lots of it. Sometimes, your child will try to use this new knowledge and ability to reason against you, baiting you into arguments. At times, he or she will inform you of facts and theories that you've never heard before. And don't be surprised if you are pushed to think deeper about certain issues and about life.

Consider it a test. To pass, remember the following simple guidelines.

Discuss; Don't Debate

Regardless of how outrageous the comment is, keep your cool. Don't be pulled into a pointless argument. Instead, appreciate your child's intellect and mental development. And have a low-key discussion of the issues.

Guide; Don't Block

Late adolescents are presented with many options for directions in life: travel, career, lifestyle, and others. This is good news, and we should celebrate the possibilities and opportunities. Consequently, they will have ideas about a wide variety of topics and choices, which can lead to some interesting discussions. Some parents have heard statements similar to these:

- "Next spring, I want to study abroad . . . in Borneo."

- "I'm thinking of changing my major to Interdisciplinary Voodoo."

- "Draco and I are considering taking a year off and backpacking through Europe."

- "Now don't get upset. I'm changing my major again. I know this is the fourth time in two years, but this time it's for good . . . I know I said that last month, but trust me, I'm sure."

You can imagine others.

At times like these, you need to fall back on the tried and true response—guide, don't block. In other words, if possible, instead of absolutely forbidding a certain course of action or dismissing it as a hair-brained, adolescent pipedream, keep calm, listen carefully, ask lots of questions, and hope the child sees the way through. Only then suggest other, more reasonable options. This won't be easy, and you will need creativity, quick thinking, and extemporaneous speaking skills, but try it.

Of course, blocking is appropriate if the son or daughter is on the verge of making a potentially disastrous decision. But for every other situation, we need to proceed with caution.

And let's be sure we answer this important question: whose needs are being met? I have seen parents pressure their children into all sorts of activities, lessons, and courses of study that have little to do with that child's interests or abilities. Sadly, the parents were meeting their own needs through their kids. The parents wanted to have a star performer in the family and the accompanying notoriety.

I've also seen Christian moms and dads struggle with a son or daughter's decision to go into the ministry. Even though two decades earlier they had stood at the front of the church and said they wanted only God's best for the child and were giving the child back to him, actually doing that is much tougher.

Listen; Don't Lecture

If you're like me, for virtually every topic you have a well-thought-out position that you're willing to share at a moment's notice. It's a sermon—three points and a poem—a lecture. But, as you probably have already discovered, preaching isn't very effective with adolescents.

So, discipline yourself, show restraint, hold your tongue, and listen. That's right, listen, really listen, *actively*—making eye contact, leaning into the conversation, responding with an occasional "hmmm" and "sure," and focusing on what is being said. For example, when the child has finished presenting his or her case for solving the world's social ills, try to repeat or clarify clearly and respectfully what you heard him or her say.

When we listen, we treat the other person with respect. It's the way we like be treated, right? And if we want our kids to act like adults (which they are becoming before our very eyes), then we should begin treating them like adults. Remember: listening is the language of love.

Keep at It

At first these attempts at talking, learning, and doing may seem awkward, almost contrived. But soon they will feel natural. Don't expect your son or daughter to respond immediately with adultlike maturity. He or she is in transition and won't know how to react, for a while, to this new place and role in life.

Also, don't expect too much too soon. The goal should be to eventually (in a few years) enjoy an adult relationship with your child. In the meantime, you will see glimpses of the little child you once knew and then the opposite—immaturity followed by signs of increased maturity. Sometimes those abrupt changes in behavior and attitudes can be unnerving and discouraging, but don't despair. Your child really is growing up—keep at it.

I can't help but worry. When you're out of sight and out of mind, I will wonder if you remember every bit of advice, every warning I've given you. How do I know whether I've shaped you at all? Maybe I've done nothing but make you want to run from my counsel and training. My worst nightmare is that you can't wait to get out from under my authority and try everything I ever prohibited you from doing. . . .

What I should do, of course, is remember those times when you were generous, when you gave of yourself, when you sacrificed, when you showed a spark of the divine. For that I would like to take credit, too, but in my fear and timidity I will be forced to attribute those qualities to the God who saved you. I will not make the mistake of ascribing to you some innate goodness apart from him, and my prayer is that I will merely be able to have confidence in your decision-making wisdom.

Jerry Jenkins, *As You Leave Home* (Colorado Springs, CO: Focus on the Family Publishing, 1993), 14–15.

CONTROLLING YOUR WORRIES

You may find it strange to find a section on "worry" in a chapter about a child's becoming an adult. But worry and fear come with that territory. We care about what is valuable to us, what we love. So our worries for our children are natural, and they show how much we care for them. As they now leave our protection, guidance, and support, we worry if they can make it on their own, and we wonder how they will invest their resources and use their freedom. We hope they will become self-supporting, responsible, and contributing members of society—adults. But, to be frank, we have our doubts.

Some of those fears may be well founded because of choices made and actions taken by our children in the past. Recently a mom told me, "I'm worried that John will do something stupid. One day I'll get a call and he'll say something like, 'Jim and I decided to go to Las Vegas for the weekend.'" Other concerns involve spending choices, study habits, social calendar, and even safety.

Unfortunately, these worries, concerns, and fears can paralyze us or tempt us to tighten our grip. Instead, we need to control those fears, voicing concerns when appropriate but continuing to release our maturing children.

As we discussed in chapter 3, release always involves risk. We'll never get to the place of total assurance that our children will always make the right decisions and will always be completely safe and sound. But we need to move from control to trust. And that's not easy. Yet that is precisely where moving to a peer relationship with our graduates begins.

Trust God. Trust yourself. Trust your child.

CONVERSATIONS

It's a difficult truth to accept, but your child is nearly an adult. Not long ago, you were kissing "owies," teaching to tie shoes,

---

WHEN FEARING THE FUTURE, REMEMBER THE PAST!

Psalm 25:6—"Remember, O LORD, your unfailing love and compassion, which you have shown from long ages past."

Psalm 42:6, 8—"Now I am deeply discouraged, but I will remember your kindness. . . . Through each day the LORD pours his unfailing love upon me, and through each night I sing his songs, praying to God who gives me life."

Psalm 77:11–12—"I recall all you have done, O LORD; I remember your wonderful deeds of long ago. They are constantly in my thoughts. I cannot stop thinking about them."

Psalm 102:25–28—"In ages past you laid the foundation of the earth, and the heavens are the work of your hands. Even they will perish, but you remain forever; they will wear out like old clothing. You will change them like a garment, and they will fade away. But you are always the same; your years never end. The children of your people will live in security. Their children's children will thrive in your presence."

Isaiah 25:1—"O LORD, I will honor and praise your name, for you are my God. You do such wonderful things! You planned them long ago, and now you have accomplished them."

---

talking to teachers at open house, cheering in the stands, and helping with homework. So how's this transition going?

1. What "significant experience" can you share with your graduate?

2. When have you had the opportunity to "guide, not block"? How did it work out?

3. What can you do to have an enjoyable and significant conversation with your son or daughter?

4. In what ways have you seen your graduate developing in his or her ability to think and reason?

5. In what areas or topics do you think you might be tempted to argue with your son or daughter next year? What do you think you will be able to do to lower the heat and discuss rationally, instead?

6. What causes you to worry about your soon-to-be-released child? What will you do to control those worries?

How come it takes so little time for a child who is afraid of the dark to become a teenager who wants to stay out all night?
—Unknown

Chapter 8

DEALING WITH INCREASED FREEDOMS

Speaking of worry, perhaps parents' greatest cause for concern is the new freedom the child will enjoy. Almost immediately the recent high school graduate's personal freedom and rights will increase considerably. Eighteen-year-olds can vote, get married, and enlist in the army.

When kids live at home, we parents usually have a pretty good idea where they are and what they are doing. We set the rules; we're in charge. On the college campus, on the military base, or in the community, it's a different story because they are far away from our watchful eyes and restricting rules.

This increase in freedom and independence is a big change for the late adolescent. It can be a heady experience, but it also can be frightening.

NEW OPTIONS

One adult "privilege" is the freedom to join the military, to defend our country. When I was growing up, young men were drafted into the service. We had to register for the draft and then, unless we had an exemption or deferment, we had to serve a minimum of two years. With the draft hanging over their heads, many young men chose to continue their education for the deferment or to fulfill their military requirement in other ways.

With an all-volunteer army, things have changed. Now recruiters for the various services work hard at filling the ranks. And many colleges and universities offer varieties of ROTC.

Whether or not your child moves in this direction, it's an adult option open to him or her.

Other options include marriage (depending on the state, allowed without parental consent at age eighteen) and full-time employment. Some kids decide to get a job, a car, and their own apartment. Many do this for a while and then continue their education.

High school grads see a whole world opening up to them. But this brings us to an important question: Who's in charge? Who makes the decisions?

NEW SUPERVISION

When our children are young, decision making abides on our turf. Imagine the diets and related health issues if our small children were allowed to choose what food to eat and what time to go to bed. We set mealtimes, playtimes, and bedtimes, and we control the schedule.

With our son Warren, it was more like a tornado effect than leaving home. That is, he comes and goes and leaves a trail of wreckage behind.

Warren had made some bad choices during high school that had us rightly concerned about his future. Although he convinced us that he would do well at a college away from home, we had our doubts. We decided to give him his shot at it anyway despite the lump in our throats, not to mention the one in our hearts. We asked one thing of Warren, as a concession on his part, and that was to spend the summer at a Christian retreat near the school so that he could, hopefully, get plugged into the right group this time. Well, since Warren takes after me, he's rather impulsive. The camp worked out all right—so much so that he was convinced to delay college and go to Youth With A Mission for an undetermined amount of time. That sounded good, except when he got to the Australia part! Being so worn out by him over the previous few years, we were open to anything that could possibly be from God.

He went, and a lot happened in the year and a half he was there. He is currently back home and pursuing college.

Ron DiCianni

As children grow, however, we have to adjust in all of those areas. Kids become increasingly less dependent upon us as they mature and learn a wide variety of life skills. We expect them to; it's part of growing up. They also make more and more of the decisions that affect their lives. As mentioned previously, our role evolves into "coach" and then into "consultant" as we give them options and encourage them to make their own choices. The number and nature of the choices varies among families, but most high school graduates probably have been given increasing amounts of freedom through the years to choose and to take responsibility for their actions. In fact, the value that increases most during adolescence is, "to make my own decisions."

So we arrive at an important juncture. Our children, now high school grads and embarking upon this new and exciting stage in life, will need to make even more decisions themselves. At the same time, however, we still should have some say in certain matters. Thus we come to this first question of supervision.

NEW DECISIONS

If the son or daughter is embarking on a career in the military, the government will handle most of the decisions about housing, daily activities, responsibilities, education, and geography.

For the college student, however, many of those decisions will rest on his or her shoulders. So who decides what courses the boy or girl will take—his or her major? You've probably already discussed this to some extent when you were choosing the institution, but believe me, it's not over. Often freshmen walk onto the university campus with ideas of pushing toward a prized career . . . until they struggle in a class or two. I've heard many say something like, "I was pre-med till I took biology" or, "I was a psych major until that statistics class." You can probably think of examples in many other fields. A dad recently told me (with much frustration in his voice) that he thinks his son holds the

COLLEGE QUESTIONS

As kids go through college, they face an onslaught of concerns and queries about themselves and where they are headed in life. These are the dominant questions for each year. They're normal—your student and the questions—so be prepared, and don't despair.

- Freshman year—"What am I doing?"
  Typical freshmen wander a lot; they also wonder. Eventually they find their way around.
- Sophomore year—"What am I doing here?" Disillusionment hits this year, and students ponder transferring to another institution where surely the grass is greener.
- Junior year—"What can I do with my major?" Literature, philosophy, or "multimedia studies" seemed right at the time, but what happens after graduation when bills have to be paid? At this point, many switch to more marketable majors.
- Senior year—"Who will I marry?" Sometime in this year, the scary thought intrudes, "Hey, my real purpose for coming here was to find a husband/wife, and I'm not even seriously dating!"—along with senior panic. Suddenly "deep" relationships spring up all over campus.

speed record for dropping a course: one hour. After attending just one class in this particular subject, the college freshman decided that he'd rather not take that course. Changing majors and career paths is normal, certainly, but at the time the change can feel devastating to the parents.

Many students have no idea at all of what to take or where to go, so they move one way and then reverse direction and go another. They may change majors five or more times in four years!

This can be maddening for us parents. We want our kids to be happy and to do well in college. But we also have a practical, pragmatic side that says, "Eventually you're going to have to get a job!" And we're not too sure that "Contemporary Studies" or

"Interdisciplinary Relational Organization" are marketable majors.

So who makes the decisions about the major and other potential life-altering choices? Or, perhaps a better question is: what's the process for making those decisions? Regardless of the question, this is an issue to talk through beforehand.

Another important topic of discussion concerns extracurricular activities: on campus and in the community. Most parents believe, and rightly so, that studies should be the top priority and should come first. That sounds good, and our students will be more than happy to agree with us. But often the classes and course work get pushed down on the priority ladder, well below fun and relationships.

Friends

When a child leaves home, he or she also leaves behind childhood relationships—friends and romances. Then, in the new environment, the young adult establishes new friendships. This can provide an interesting challenge to the folks back home.

When our children were very young, most of their playmates lived in the neighborhood. Then they made friends with kids at church and school. Eventually, as teenagers, these friendships became more intense, and our kids grew interested in the opposite sex. Certainly, all those relationships had their ups and downs—peer pressure, moral dilemmas, dating rules and rituals, and so forth. They made for some interesting conversations and conflicts at home. But at least we knew something about the principal characters in the play. The friends and dates lived in our community and went to the same high school as our kids. Usually we knew their parents.

Away from the neighborhood, school, and church—far away—our children will find new boys and girls (men and women) to hang with. Often these new associates will come from distant states or even far-off lands. The only information we will have about them will come from our kids. This will necessitate trust and open communication.

Regarding romance, graduates often must leave high school sweethearts behind. For some, this is traumatic and may even affect the college student's studies and grades. Usually these relationships fade after a few months as everyone moves on. If not, you may need to have a heart-to-heart talk with your student, reminding him or her of the high priority of doing well in school.

Dating

And what about relationships with the opposite sex and potential sexual involvement? Not to increase your anxiety, but here's another area of great temptation for single, available, and normal young people, away from home and making their own decisions. They fall within the category of "consenting adults."

The pressure to have sex is tremendous, especially on certain campuses and in certain peer groups. Our society's obsession with all things sexual exacerbates the pressure and problem. When popular music, movies, and TV shows, celebrities, news media, and even politicians seem to promote promiscuity, it's easy to buy into the lie that sleeping around is okay and doesn't hurt anyone.

Trust me; your son or daughter will face strong temptation in this area.

Entertainment

Compared to the previous couple of areas and temptations, this will seem minor. But it's another change and an important one.

Up till now, you probably have had fairly strict rules about what to watch on TV, how to use the Internet, and what DVDs to rent and movies to see. Again, away from your direct influence and supervision (and away from the home church and Christian peer group), your son or daughter will be free to move away from those restrictions.

How our kids respond to all of these temptations will depend, for the most part, on what they have already learned and internalized. That is, if they have a moral compass—they know right from wrong and intend to do what is right—they will stand strong and stay the course.

On the other hand, if they tend to be easily influenced by peers and circumstances, they may be blown about by every prevailing moral wind.

Drinking

Now here's a sticky one. Sure, in high school many kids drink, but it's illegal. So that's always a trump card that parents can play regardless of any other moral considerations. But when our kids are away from home, out of our sight and supervision, they will be making their own decisions in this area.

In the United States, the minimum age for legally consuming alcoholic beverages is twenty-one, except for educational, religious, or medical purposes. So in a few years, our recent high school graduates will cross that threshold. But drinking by college students, soldiers and sailors, and others between eighteen and twenty-one is well known and, according to some, epidemic. Regardless of where our kids end up, they will face pressure to drink.

If they attend a Christian college or university, alcohol use probably will be prohibited. Thus, if for no other reason, they shouldn't drink simply because it would be against the rules. But they still will be tempted to indulge—it comes with the territory.

As I have stated repeatedly (because it's important to remember), our ultimate goal for our children is to see them become fully functioning, autonomous, and mature adults. Then, hopefully, we will relate to them as fellow adults, almost as peers.

We always will be their parents, of course, but our roles and relationships will have matured and changed.

This will be a good topic for another talk with your son or daughter. Explain that you are well aware of his or her new freedom; that is, you won't be around to monitor activities, comings and goings, and relationships. As one dad has put it in talking with his son, "You will have to build your own guardrails." Then express your trust in your son or daughter, reaffirming some of the statements that you made in your blessing. You may also want to reiterate your pleasure in seeing him or her become an adult. Explain that you realize the fear that can accompany freedom and growing up but that you are confident in his or her ability to make it in this next stage of life.

CONVERSATIONS

One of the biggest changes for the recent graduate is his or her new freedom. Away from the direct supervision of Mom and Dad, the child makes decisions concerning time, relationships, entertainment, and many other choices. How do you feel about this independence?

1. In the last three years, what big decision have you made for your son or daughter? What big decisions have you allowed him or her to make?

2. What important decisions will you allow him or her to make in the next year or two?

3. How do you feel about your son or daughter's increased freedom? What evidence do you have that he or she will make positive and responsible decisions?

4. What do you think will be your son or daughter's greatest moral temptation? What steps can you take now to help prepare him or her for those tempting times?

5. How will you respond if your child makes poor decisions?

If your outgo exceeds your income, then your upkeep will be your downfall.
—Unknown

Chapter 9

HANDLING FINANCES

Before your son or daughter leaves home, you'll need to have "the talk." No, not about the birds and the bees (hopefully you covered that years ago), but about money.

Everyone is familiar with the saying, "Money is the root of all evil." But that's a poor paraphrase of the beginning of 1 Timothy 6:10. That verse actually is, "For the love of money is at the root of all kinds of evil." Then Paul continues. "And some people, craving money, have wandered from the faith and pierced themselves with many sorrows." So money isn't the issue; it's the *love* of money, the craving for money, and the misuse of money that cause the problems. In fact, one of the leading sources of relational conflict is money—especially in families. So you'll need to have that talk with your graduate if you want to keep your relationship strong.

Talking about money is especially important at this time because it relates directly to the issues of freedom and being a responsible adult.

BILL PAYING

So that leads to an important question: Who pays the bills?

Although we hate to admit this, sometimes the bottom line for us really is money. Or at least that's what we communicate with phrases like "As long as I'm paying the bills . . . " or "When you get a job and have money of your own, then you'll be able to make those decisions. But for now . . . "

No wonder some kids want to have jobs during high school so that they can have their own money, to spend as they please.

Parenthetically, I'm not a big fan of students working in high school, during the academic year. Although parents will often say, "Having a job teaches kids how to be responsible and how to manage money," often the result is the opposite. That is, working adolescents learn how to *waste* money. I could say much more on this (see my book *Tough Parents for Tough Times*), but my point is simply that regardless of the source of our children's income (allowance, money from us for extra work, part-time jobs in the neighborhood or elsewhere, or gifts), we should help them see the big picture—how their income is part of the *family* financial pool and not just theirs to spend however they want.

What if, for example, each person in the family had the attitude that he or she could use all earned income as he or she wished, on him- or herself? Dad's paycheck goes to Dad alone. Mom's paycheck goes to her alone. The same applies to each of the children. If that happened, the family would fall apart—it just wouldn't work. And the parents probably would be arrested for child endangerment. No—responsible, adult parents realize that all of the income belongs to the family, to be used wisely. And Christian parents realize that, in reality, it all belongs to God who has given them the responsibility to be good stewards. So instead of selfishly demanding control of every penny, as contributing family members we learn to share, to work together on the family economy, and to use well the resources entrusted to us.

That's a long-winded speech, but here's the point: our children need to understand how all of this works and how they are contributors, not just takers, in the process. Hopefully, over the past several years, they have learned how to save money and may even have a sizeable amount in their "college fund." Now that they are ready to take that next step, those funds can be used for their intended purpose.

FINANCIAL PLANS

Families differ in their philosophies concerning how to finance college. Some leave that entirely up to the student. In that case, he or she has to patch together a financial plan that combines savings, grants/scholarships, employment at school, and loans. Some parents stand at the other end of the spectrum and pay almost all the bills—tuition, room, board, and so forth—and expect their kids to cover only spending money. Many fall somewhere in between.

In one family, a pastor's son wanted to go to a private Christian college. That sounded great except that private colleges are very expensive, and pastors don't receive high salaries. Fortunately for this family, the college had the policy of giving a 33 percent tuition discount to families in Christian ministry. So the pastor and his son agreed to split the balance. That is, the father and mother would pay for half of the remaining amount owed to the college, and the son would be responsible for the balance. It worked! The son, however, graduated with a fairly large student loan to repay.

Many parents plan ahead and save money every month in a "college fund" for each child. Then they pay for everything related to the academic side of college (tuition, room, board, books, fees, travel to and from school, and so forth), while the child is responsible for his or her spending money. Parents may offer to add to the spending money fund the amount reduced by schol-

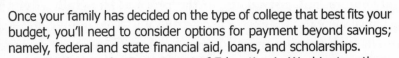

Once your family has decided on the type of college that best fits your budget, you'll need to consider options for payment beyond savings; namely, federal and state financial aid, loans, and scholarships.

According to the Department of Education in Washington, there is $60 billion available for educational aid. While you won't require quite that much for your child's education, you may want to invest the time to see exactly how much you could receive in aid.

The first place to start when thinking about financial aid for your education is the FAFSA (Free Application for Federal Student Aid) form. This is the form you need to fill out to get any federal assistance. The form helps to determine your EFC (Estimated Family Contribution).

Christopher D. Hudson, et. al. *Money Clues for the Clueless* (Uhrichsville, OH: Promise Press, 2000), 123.

arships and grants for the areas that they would be underwriting.

In some families, Mom and Dad explain early on that they will contribute a set amount toward the college education, with the expectation that the student will make up the difference. That amount may be high or low, depending on the college or university choice.

Students with financial responsibilities, then, get their funds by working in the summers, working on or near the campus, serving as a resident hall advisor (usually that provides free housing), obtaining scholarships or grants, taking out a loan, or a combination.

Whatever direction you take, remember these simple points:

1. Have a plan! Decide what you want to do and then talk it through with your student. After getting input (ideas, feelings, thoughts) from your son or daughter, design that plan as specifically as possible. The plan should answer these questions: How much will be paid by whom? How will the payments be made? When will the payments be made?

2. Work the plan! Hold yourself and your child accountable for making the plan work.

3. Adjust the plan! No plan should be chiseled in stone because circumstances change. You may be surprised positively or negatively by what you learn as your child progresses through college. So discuss regularly how the plan is working and evaluate it annually or semi-annually.

Unless you have decided that your child is totally on his or her own at this point and, thus, has total control over all of the financial decisions, let me make a couple of suggestions.

MY MONEY VS. OUR MONEY

First, settle the issue of "my money" versus "our money." Explain that you consider this a partnership, that you're in it together. Talk through, thoroughly, the funding plan and your expectations for your son or daughter related to the plan. Here, topics like budget, stewardship, and accountability should be covered. See this as a team effort, and remember that your goal is to have your son or daughter learn how to handle money responsibly and be able to support him- or herself in the world.

LETTER FROM COLLEGE:

Dear Dad,

    $chool i$ really great. I've made lot$ of friend$ and am $studying hard. With all my $tuff, I $imply can't think of anything I need. $o if you would like, you can ju$t $end me a card, a$ I would love to hear from you.

Love,
Your $on

REPLY FROM DAD

Dear Son,

    I kNOw that astroNOmy, and oceaNOgraphy are eNOugh to keep even an hoNOr student busy. Do NOt forget that the pursuit of kNOwledge is a NOble task, and you can never study hard eNOugh.

Love,
Dad

From "Mikey's Funnies": www.mikeysfunnies.com

A college housemate of mine remarked one day that he hated the cafeteria food and that from now on he would be eating in restaurants. I asked how he could afford that and why he would even consider doing that when his meals were already paid for. He answered that he had a job and it was *his* money, so he could do what he wanted with it. I was shocked because I knew his parents had paid for the meal plan. I also knew that my mom and dad had sacrificed to send me to college and that whatever I earned as a student would take pressure off them. Unfortunately, my friend had a much different view.

MONEY WITH STRINGS ATTACHED

Second, be honest about any strings attached to finances. Long before my daughters were ready for college, I wondered about how I would feel writing those huge tuition checks. Years later, however, when I had to do just that, I found the experience to be relatively painless. In fact, I considered it a privilege to be able to invest in their lives. Paying for college didn't feel much different than when I paid for piano lessons or summer camp. The amount of investment was much larger certainly, but the feelings were similar.

On the other hand, suppose I had written the check (say, for example, for $20,000), and my daughter had messed around, goofed off, and done very poorly in her classes. I think I would have felt differently about the experience. So did I have "strings attached" to my generosity? As much as I hate to admit it, I probably did.

Some parents seem to enjoy controlling their kids with money. But that's not healthy. It certainly doesn't help young people become independent.

So I'll say it again: be honest about your financial strings. You will be investing heavily in your child, especially if he or she is entering college. You hope, however, that eventually your adult

FINANCIAL NOTES

- Watch out for dorm theft. Don't assume that everyone is as honest as your son or daughter, regardless of the school.
- A huge financial burden can come from cell phone bills.
- Students can save big bucks by purchasing textbooks in used books sales or online. They should check www.CheapestTextbooks.com and other Web sites.

child will be a fully functioning, self-sustaining, and contributing member of society, financially independent from you and paying his or her own bills.

So talk about your expectations. Kids need to know the money that they and their parents have worked hard to accumulate for this moment, the funds they have sacrificed to put together, should not be taken lightly or squandered. On the other hand, we shouldn't threaten to drop our support over small indiscretions, mistakes, and letdowns, letting our emerging adults think that our financial investment means we will control every action. We need to give them freedom, and this includes freedom to fail.

Giving freedom here won't be easy because as much as we don't want to believe this about ourselves, money often motivates our actions. That's why we must keep the goal in sight: helping our children become autonomous—positively and truly letting go.

REASONABLE EXPECTATIONS

So what are your expectations? If your child is getting married or moving to a new job miles away, then he or she will be self-supporting very soon. Most college students, however, are in transition. For the next four years, or more, their housing, meals, insurance, and related services will be chosen by parents and the college administration.

Life on a college or university campus can provide great

learning experiences beyond the classrooms, but usually not in the area of personal finance. But it can be—if you make it so. With careful planning, you can prepare your son or daughter for life as an adult, after getting that prized degree.

But first, here's a warning: beware of the assault of the credit card companies. Visa, MasterCard, and others make it very easy for students to get cards, even though these young people have not established any credit history. That may seem foolish, but it's actually very shrewd because the companies know that caring parents stand behind the students and will bail them out of their credit card debts. So here's my advice: don't allow your son or daughter to have a credit card (or debit card) while in college.

You've probably seen the TV specials on college students and credit, and the facts are appalling. Many students pile up massive credit card debts and then are surprised to receive the bills. Others use cards knowing that bills will arrive but are shocked when charged interest for the unpaid balances.

So as you discuss college finances with your student, begin by explaining that you want him or her to have the necessary funds but that you also want him or her to learn how to manage money.

WISDOM FROM PROVERBS ON MONEY

- "It is possible to give freely and become more wealthy, but those who are stingy will lose everything. The generous prosper and are satisfied; those who refresh others will themselves be refreshed" (Proverbs 11:24–25).
- "It is poor judgment to co-sign a friend's note, to become responsible for a neighbor's debts" (Proverbs 17:18).
- "The wise have wealth and luxury, but fools spend whatever they get" (Proverbs 21:20).
- "Just as the rich rule the poor, so the borrower is servant to the lender" (Proverbs 22:7).
- "Do not co-sign another person's note or put up a guarantee for someone else's loan. If you can't pay it, even your bed will be snatched from under you" (Proverbs 22:26–27).

Then, as mentioned earlier, be honest about your "strings" (what you expect) and the priority of studies.

Let your student know how many years you will be financing. That is, if you expect him or her to finish in four years, say so.

And be sure to discuss accounting and accountability. For example, you may want your student to design a budget and then keep a good record of his or her income and expenses. As he or she demonstrates maturity and responsibility, you can give him or her more freedom. If not, then you won't. This lives out the biblical principle of stewardship: "Unless you are faithful in small matters, you won't be faithful in large ones" (Luke 16:10).

TRIAL RUN

Hopefully by now you have taught your child the important life skills related to finances: how to save money, how to design a budget, how to shop, and so forth. To make sure that he or she is ready for this next phase of life, take this training to the next level with a trial run.

Some parents do this for their student's senior year in high school—the whole year. But you can do it for a shorter period of time. The idea is to live as though it is the first year after high school. Here's how it works.

First, sit down and discuss the purpose for your course of action: you want your student to be disciplined and able to make good financial decisions. Then explain the process and the ground rules. You might say this, for example:

- "You need to go to a bank and set up a checking account for you. We will help you do this if you want us to" (if the student doesn't already have an account).

- "We will deposit into your account all of the money

that we have budgeted for your expenses, not including food, for the next three months" (or shorter if
you don't have three months).

- "Normally, this money would cover the costs of your
  clothes, entertainment, school fees, spending money,
  and other expenses, but you can save it or spend it
  anyway you want."

- "When the money runs out, that's it."

- "You need to keep track of how you spend the
  money. You can use your checkbook, a computer
  program, a ledger, or another system. But after
  these three months, we will go over it with you to
  see what we can learn."

Then, tell the amount of money and give it to your son or
daughter to deposit into his or her account. Your child should
open the account if he or she doesn't already have one.

Make sure you follow the plan yourself. Don't give in to tearful
pleas for money for the social event that he or she just *has* to attend,
since funds that could have paid for it were spent on an iPod or
computer game.

At the end of the quarter, go over the record with your child,
noting the amounts spent for which categories. Ask about the
lessons your son or daughter learned and what he or she will do
differently next time. At some point, be sure to show how this is,
in fact, a trial run, practice for the next year.

This can be a great learning experience.

Don't allow the issue of money to divide the family. Instead,
use it to teach your son or daughter adult skills. Everyone will
be better off.

JESUS ON MONEY—A SAMPLING

- Matthew 6:24—"No one can serve two masters. For you will hate one and love the other, or be devoted to one and despise the other. You cannot serve both God and money."
- Matthew 19:21–24—"Jesus told him, 'If you want to be perfect, go and sell all you have and give the money to the poor, and you will have treasure in heaven. Then come, follow me.' But when the young man heard this, he went sadly away because he had many possessions. Then Jesus said to his disciples, 'I tell you the truth, it is very hard for a rich person to get into the Kingdom of Heaven. I say it again—it is easier for a camel to go through the eye of a needle than for a rich person to enter the Kingdom of God!'"
- Matthew 21:12–13—"Jesus entered the Temple and began to drive out the merchants and their customers. He knocked over the tables of the money changers and the stalls of those selling doves. He said, 'The Scriptures declare, "My Temple will be called a place of prayer," but you have turned it into a den of thieves!'"
- Luke 6:32–34—"Do you think you deserve credit merely for loving those who love you? Even the sinners do that! And if you do good only to those who do good to you, is that so wonderful? Even sinners do that much! And if you lend money only to those who can repay you, what good is that? Even sinners will lend to their own kind for a full return."
- Luke 16:10–12—"Unless you are faithful in small matters, you won't be faithful in large ones. If you cheat even a little, you won't be honest with greater responsibilities. And if you are untrustworthy about worldly wealth, who will trust you with the true riches of heaven? And if you are not faithful with other people's money, why should you be trusted with money of your own?"

CONVERSATIONS

Money seems central to just about every aspect of our lives. No wonder the pursuit of it, the saving of it, and the spending of it cause so much conflict. Thus learning how to manage money is an important life skill for anyone to have, especially someone just beginning his or her way in the world. And that includes a financial strategy for the future.

1. What plan do you have in place for handling your son or daughter's financial burdens over the next few years?

2. What strings have you attached to your financial involvement? What are your expectations for your son or daughter?

3. When did you learn financial life skills? What hard lessons did you learn along the way?

4. In what ways has your child demonstrated maturity in handling money? What does he or she still have to learn in this area?

5. What will you do to teach your graduate what he or she needs to learn to be prepared for next year?

*Never doubt in
darkness what God has
shown you in the light.*
—V. Raymond Edman

Chapter 10

KEEPING THE
FAITH

A couple millennia ago, the apostle Paul wrote, "It's like this: When I was a child, I spoke and thought and reasoned as a child does. But when I grew up, I put away childish things" (1 Corinthians 13:11). Kids are still growing up and putting away any and all evidences of childhood. This happens for a number of reasons—physical changes, for example. I mean, have you ridden your Big Wheel lately? Often, however, our reasons and motivations are much more subtle and even subconscious. As we move to a new life plateau, we leave behind the symbols of the previous one. Remember when you entered high school? You probably carried few, if any, junior high symbols with you. You had moved on.

You may have experienced something similar in college. I know I did. During the first few days of freshmen orientation, I saw guys wearing high school letter jackets (myself included). Some students even had honor society pins and other awards on them. But only for a day or so. Quickly those former status symbols were stored away, and if the jackets were worn, the athletic letters had been removed. We were now college students and had left high school in the dust.

This feeling of moving on and away from childhood's toys, activities, and symbols can touch more sensitive areas, including church and faith. And this can be tough for Mom and Dad to deal with. But we need to remember that adolescents are changing in every area of life. They are maturing spiritually too (and that's good).

Environmental Christians

Perhaps you can identify with my experience.

I was an "environmental Christian." I had been reared in a wonderful Christian home and had been heavily involved in a strong evangelical church. In fact, at times I was more zealous in my witnessing and separation from the world than either my parents or the church had promoted. I had made a profession of faith in Christ as my "personal Savior" at the ripe old age of seven (my mother had prayed with me after a Child Evangelism Fellowship meeting in our home), and I had been immersed in church activities all my life (Sunday school, Daily Vacation Bible School, church camp, Youth for Christ rallies and clubs, choir, prayer meeting, Sunday evening service, youth group meetings and activities, and so forth).

To put it mildly, I was confident in what I believed—the *truth*—even cocky. I thought I had all the answers. Yet as a freshman at Wheaton College, a strong evangelical institution, I encountered students in my dorm who were much better Christians than I (more devotion to Christ, more Bible knowledge, and deeper spiritual life) who believed differently in certain areas. Also, from other students and in various classes, I heard questions for which I had no answers. Even more disconcerting, I discovered that I had the answers for questions no one was asking. Suddenly my *faith* began to seem very irrelevant and childish, and I began to struggle with doubts.

This experience blindsided me. My goal was Christian ministry, and I knew Wheaton would prepare me for that calling. So I was surprised and unnerved to see my belief system unravel. I began to think, "I could be wrong," "My parents could be wrong," and "My pastor could be wrong!" And I "lost" my faith. Oh, I didn't act out or become obnoxious about my new questions, but issues, doctrines, and "answers" about which I had been so confident a few months before became places of confusion and struggle.

As I said, I was an environmental Christian; that is, my Christianity had come from my environment—it wasn't my own. I had been surrounded by it, and others had given it to me. So when I left my home and Christian environment, in effect I left my faith. Soon I doubted everything: the truth of the Bible, Jesus Christ as divine, and even the existence of God.

Ironically, my journey back began at nearly the same time. At football camp, our captain spoke about keeping focused on Christ. Everyone else will let us down, he said, but Jesus never will. Later, another team leader spoke about the importance of the Resurrection. At the time, I listened with casual interest. Later, at a critical juncture, I remembered their words.

Professors also made a big impact—chapel speakers too. One said it was all right to doubt if we were looking for answers, and J. Edwin Orr spoke about "Faith That Makes Sense." (I bought his book with that title.) And I discovered C. S. Lewis and other Christian thinkers.

Through the next year or two and by God's grace and the help of dedicated Christian professors and friends, slowly, stone by stone, my faith was rebuilt, and I was able to believe again. Actually, the theological result wasn't dramatically different to what I had professed just a couple of years earlier, but this time my faith was my own!

Like thousands of other college freshmen, one of the "childish things" I had "put away" was my immature relationship with God.

If your teenager has a similar background and has not internalized and personalized his or her faith, you can expect similar struggles.

PRESSURES AND TEMPTATIONS

Parents who send kids to Christian schools often think that the values- and beliefs-friendly environment at the school will protect their children and push them to grow spiritually. Parents who see their kids go off on their own, enlist in the military, or attend a secular university often worry that their children will be pressured and tempted to deny their faith and abandon their morals.

In all situations, anything is possible because the young person is away from home and free to make his or her own choices. If your child moves to a Christian campus, don't be lulled into complacency, thinking that he or she won't be challenged or tempted. If your child moves to a secular environment, don't be worried sick that he or she will wipe out theologically and morally.

We know our kids will face pressures to act differently than they would at home, and that they will be tempted to experiment with a variety of ideas and lifestyles. As we covered in chapter 8, freedom and temptation walk hand in hand. So let your son or daughter know that you know and that you don't want anything to mess up your relationship with him or her. Encourage your son or daughter to remember who he or she is—a marvelous creation of a loving heavenly Father, one for whom Christ died and in whom the Holy Spirit resides. Your child is loved, by God and by you!

Then pray and trust God. Your son or daughter is in his hands. As Jeremiah declared: "O Sovereign LORD! You have made the heavens and earth by your great power. Nothing is too hard for you!" (Jeremiah 32:17).

Mitzie Barton explains that she prayed daily that her daughter, Kari, would find a Christian friend at her secular university. When that didn't happen the first year, Mitzie decided that God would answer her prayer in his way and in his time, and she kept

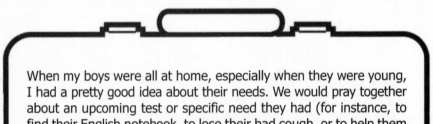

When my boys were all at home, especially when they were young, I had a pretty good idea about their needs. We would pray together about an upcoming test or specific need they had (for instance, to find their English notebook, to lose their bad cough, or to help them to be kinder to an irritating friend). As they matured, I knew less and less about their needs and desires. How do you pray for your child when you are unaware of all the specifics in his life? You can simply ask God to help him do the next right thing, whatever that may be. You see, if your child and mine will do the next right thing and follow that with the next right thing and then do the NEXT right thing, they will definitely be on the right track.

Kendra Smiley, *Helping Your Kids Make Good Choices* (Ann Arbor, MI: Servant Publications, 2000), 173.

praying. The next year, the university hired a new basketball coach—a dedicated Christian woman. Mitzie says, "At that school, that was a miracle, and a sure sign that God was taking care of my daughter."

CHURCH

Regardless of your child's destination, almost certainly he or she will adjust the church-going routines. Some of this is by choice. Other changes just happen because of circumstances.

Attendance

Those who work with college students report that most kids, even at Christian schools, don't attend church services much during their freshman year. This happens for a variety of reasons, not the least of which we have already covered in depth—freedom. When they are growing up, even if parents don't force them to go to worship services, most young people in Christian homes are expected to attend. And their parents make sure these children are up on time and dressed appropriately and have transportation. It's a family event, as it should be.

Away from home, arising early on Sunday, after a Saturday night of hanging out, partying, or goofing off, takes remarkable discipline and commitment, especially when everyone else seems to be sleeping in. In addition, no one is there to make sure these adolescents are up and ready, the closest church of interest may be miles away, and the students have no personal connections with any church. So if your son or daughter sleeps in or decides to study on Sunday mornings at first, don't panic—he or she is typical.

Just suggest to your student that plugging into a good church and Christian organization will help him or her make an easier transition to life away from home because he or she can meet other Christian students and helpful leaders. Your son or daughter will also find support, instruction, and Bible study, enabling him or her to grow in the faith.

Many denominations sponsor student groups on secular campuses. And interdenominational Christian groups like InterVarsity Christian Fellowship, Navigators, Fellowship of Christian Athletes, and Campus Crusade for Christ have chapters nationwide. Those would be good options to investigate first, for fellowship and encouragement. And suggest checking out a number of churches before settling into one. Some churches reach out to students and offer attractive programs, including transportation for those who need it. During the year, your son or daughter may connect with other Christian students who will recommend a church; then they can go together.

Put yourself in your student's shoes, and you'll be able to empathize with his or her predicament. Imagine how hard it would be for you to go to church by yourself, in a new city where you didn't know anyone. It would be doable, of course, just not

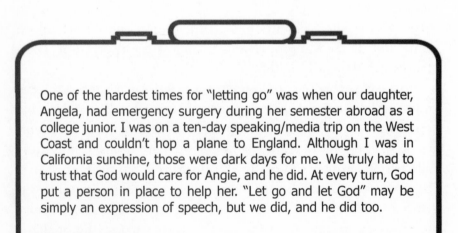

One of the hardest times for "letting go" was when our daughter, Angela, had emergency surgery during her semester abroad as a college junior. I was on a ten-day speaking/media trip on the West Coast and couldn't hop a plane to England. Although I was in California sunshine, those were dark days for me. We truly had to trust that God would care for Angie, and he did. At every turn, God put a person in place to help her. "Let go and let God" may be simply an expression of speech, but we did, and he did too.

Mary Manz Simon

easy. You would have to be very motivated to make the effort. So pray that your son or daughter connects with a strong Christian friend, coach, teacher, or small group. Positive peer pressure always helps.

Experimentation

A common area of experimentation for young people away from home and on their own involves the form of worship. And often they swing to the opposite end of the spectrum for a while.

Kids from liturgical backgrounds may begin attending those with an informal worship style—Baptist, Assemblies of God, Vineyard, or Bible churches. Or they may be drawn to independent churches meeting in very plain settings—warehouses, storefronts, or schools. In describing their experience, these students might say, "I appreciate the freedom and spontaneity. People

My husband, a pastoral counselor, has been my best source of parenting advice. He was and is always quick to remind parents that every child is an individual. They all have their own personality, they learn in their own unique ways, and they have very specific and special calls in life—all of which might be different from you or other children! So, carefully listen to the Lord regarding your children. Don't try to make them like you, and don't criticize them if they're not like you.

Pray for them every day. Make a prayer list and revise it monthly or quarterly. Pray for their friends and teachers and for their safety. No matter how far they get from you or God, don't ever be afraid to say, "I'm praying for you. I love you."

Becky Tirabassi

seem so close to God there." They enjoy seeing God as near, as a friend, and exclaim that the services are so free and the people so friendly.

Conversely, young people from informal worship settings may gravitate to Lutheran, Episcopal, or Roman Catholic churches, with stained-glass windows, candles, and robed clergy. They remark, "I love the atmosphere; it's so worshipful. I feel so close to God." They enjoy the focus on the awesomeness of God.

While those two descriptions may fit churches in certain denominations, these days a person can find a variety of worship styles within the same denomination. A Lutheran student from a very formal, traditional church, for example, might be attracted to a Lutheran church with a contemporary celebration service (and vice versa). The same could be said for Presbyterian, Methodist, Baptist, and other traditions.

Some of these denominational adjustments may be reactions to the past. Often, however, these young people are simply trying to find their own worship style, where they fit and feel connected to God. It's part of the process of personalizing faith, making it their own.

I have to warn you: while home at break, students may express strong, negative opinions about their spiritual past and the home church. Now that they have a basis for comparison, they may decide that the church of their youth doesn't measure up. Try not to react emotionally to those charged statements. Consider these tensions as growing pains. And who knows, your son or daughter may even have a point or two!

QUESTIONS, DOUBTS, AND PERSONAL FAITH

The process of learning how to think also can cause many conflicts in Christian homes as they bring home their questions. Besides worship style, they may challenge basic beliefs.

Ideas and Concepts

As we covered briefly in chapter 7, adolescents are learning to think. This comes in stages. Remember the first stage—concrete thinking? From when our kids are young, all the way into the junior high years, they think concretely. That is, they take statements literally, at face value. They don't do well with figures of speech or abstract concepts.

When I worked with middle school students, I remember telling a group (very seriously) that I used to be six foot eight. That got their attention because, although I'm tall, that seemed a bit too tall. So they responded, "What! What do you mean? How tall are you now?"

I answered, "I'm six foot three." Then, after a brief pause, I continued. "You see, I went on a strict Crisco diet."

"What?" they exclaimed. "That stuff you cook with?"

And I answered, "Yes, it's *shortening*!" (You can groan now at the joke.)

Only two kids laughed. The rest wanted to argue with me: "You can't eat that—it's greasy!" They took me literally, concretely.

That's the difference between thinking concretely and thinking

In my experience with our son's spiritual slump, I eventually reached a point where I declared hands off. Although I was desperately concerned about our son, I realized that I could become a victim, consumed by fear and a lack of trust. Of course God was interested in my son, but God also wanted to produce in me a deep trust in his faithfulness.

Jeanne Hendricks, *Mom's Devotional Bible* (Grand Rapids, MI: Zondervan Publishing House, 1996), 877.

conceptually. A few of the middle schoolers in my group (eighth graders) had made the transition, but not many.

If you've taught confirmation classes (usually with eighth graders), you've faced the same problem. The Christian faith is loaded with profound concepts: repentance, atonement, salvation, justification, sanctification, Lordship of Christ, faith, grace, and so forth. But these are very difficult for children to grasp. (No wonder church is boring!) You try your hardest to teach and explain the lesson, but your students just don't get it. In a year or two, after they've made the transition and can understand, you probably will be able to have productive and positive conversations with them on those concepts.

But learning to think conceptually is not the end of a person's intellectual development. Eventually, most adults learn to think analytically and critically. University students almost always experience this transition.

In college classes, students are expected to doubt and test various theories and points of view, to think through the issues, and to arrive at their own conclusions. Learning to analyze and then having informed, and strong, opinions can be painful for both the student and parents.

As mentioned previously, nothing is more frustrating for parents than young people discovering their minds—students who have had one psychology or philosophy course and think they have everything figured out. Anticipate that your child will come home from college and argue with you about politics, social justice, racial prejudice, and, even, theology. Dealing with students who are learning to think on their own, to form their own opinions, can be annoying.

When this happens, when your student makes an inflammatory remark or spouts the latest psychobabble, do your best to listen quietly and respectfully and try not to get into an argument. Try to make your first response positive, saying something like, "That's interesting." Look for something to affirm in what he or she says, and let your son or daughter know that you respect his or her opinion. Then, if you disagree with what has been stated, ask clarification questions to help your student come to a conclusion before you give your opinion. This helps avoid turning the discussion into an "I think/you think" situation. Then give a few thoughts, facts, and ideas on the other side of the argument for him or her to think about. One woman explained that she would always come home with extremely liberal ideas, echoing her professors at the university. She and her father would argue, but he never got upset with her. He simply would counter with conservative answers and cause her to think through her position.

Often parents wonder what their child's professors are teaching them in college. But if you patiently allow your child to think and to work through new and challenging ideas, you can keep a close relationship.

I need to add that the crazy ideas or weird theological pronouncements might not accurately represent the professors' viewpoints. In fact, I remember Kara calling me from college one evening, all upset at something she thought her professor had been teaching in her Christian Thought class. When I pointed out that Dr. Johnson probably was just trying to get her to think (a good assumption, considering the title of the class), she calmed down. So don't fly to the university to rescue your child from the evil educators.

When I was a boy of fourteen, my father was so ignorant I could hardly stand to have the old man around. But when I got to be twenty-one, I was astonished at how much the old man had learned in seven years.

Mark Twain—http://festivals.iloveindia.com/fathers-day/fathers-day-quotes.html

Doubts

With all of this critical thinking and questioning will come doubts. No one is immune to doubting, not even young people who are well grounded in solid theology. That is, their faith has matured along with their maturation physically, socially, mentally, and emotionally. And if we were honest, we would have to admit that doubts aren't the exclusive domain of college students. They dog everyone.

Some doubts are triggered from outside by challenges from professors and others. They can also arise inside as we struggle with serious questions and issues. Sometimes life's circumstances push or pull us that way: the death of a dream or a loved one, a serious setback or accident, or another personal or global catastrophe. "Where is God?" we may cry. "How could he let this happen?"

Some people keep quiet, hiding their questions. Others voice their doubts loudly, as angry challenges to God. As the parent of a late adolescent who is learning how to think critically and to express his or her thoughts, you may hear a few of those challenges.

Remember the spiritual response to horrors of 9/11 and Hurricane Katrina and other devastating disasters? Many doubts about God's goodness and sovereignty were voiced from all quarters. Yet, these catastrophes drove people to prayer, to church, to God, and to selfless service in Christ's name.

When you hear those questions and challenges to your faith, whether from intellectual curiosity or from the heart, try not to react. And please don't say, "Christians don't doubt!" Instead, you might want to point out that the questions are good. When you get the chance, explain that it's all right to doubt—everyone does—but we should look for answers. Encourage your son or daughter to become an "honest seeker" instead of a "professional doubter."

I know that I don't have all the answers. And I have a bunch of questions that I'm planning to ask God when I get to heaven. But one truth that has helped me during my times of questioning is that none of these questions catch God by surprise. He doesn't exclaim, "Oh no! What about those natives who have never heard about Christ? What am I going to do about them?" I know God is loving and just. I also know that I'm not him—my intellect is very limited.

This won't be easy to do, but try to see the presence of doubts and questions as a good sign. Your son or daughter is growing up and is honest.

The challenges to faith are the most difficult for us to take in stride. Actually, this process of thinking through what they believe is good, but that doesn't make it easy to deal with. When our kids seem to be rejecting their church, doubting many of their foundational beliefs, and talking openly about strange philosophies and theological tangents, we will be tempted to argue back. That's when we must exercise restraint, encouraging our students to keep looking for answers and remembering that, "A gentle answer turns away wrath, but harsh words stir up anger" (Proverbs 15:1).

Eventually, especially after they have taken a few more courses and experienced a bit more of life, they will mellow and may even agree with you and your opinions. And having a faith that is actually theirs is good.

Remember, too, that if you've done a good job in modeling Christian values, teaching life skills, and building a solid faith foundation, your son or daughter won't throw everything overboard and join a cult. I know that my girls were much better prepared to build their faith and deal with doubts because of the outstanding youth ministry at our church. During high school they were exposed to C. S. Lewis, Francis Schaeffer, Ravi Zaccharias, and other Christian apologists whom I didn't discover until college and beyond.

STRETCHED FAITH

Talk is cheap. And nowhere is talk cheaper than in the Christian life. We stand and sing with gusto, "I surrender all," "You are my all in all," "In Christ alone I take my stand," and other songs of devotion. We memorize verses about faith. We even testify that we love God more than anything and trust him with everything. But do we really? How we react to giving up what is most precious to us will reveal the truth. So while we may wonder about our children's questioning and rediscovering and redefining their faith, we will do a little faith stretching of our own.

Sending that precious son or daughter off into the world is a true test of faith, and it provides a great opportunity to live what we profess to believe, to truly release our child to God's care. Because we love our children desperately, we want them to be safe and secure—and we pray for that. The old cliché becomes true: we must "let go and let God."

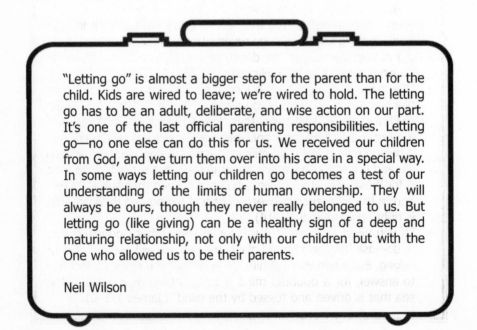

"Letting go" is almost a bigger step for the parent than for the child. Kids are wired to leave; we're wired to hold. The letting go has to be an adult, deliberate, and wise action on our part. It's one of the last official parenting responsibilities. Letting go—no one else can do this for us. We received our children from God, and we turn them over into his care in a special way. In some ways letting our children go becomes a test of our understanding of the limits of human ownership. They will always be ours, though they never really belonged to us. But letting go (like giving) can be a healthy sign of a deep and maturing relationship, not only with our children but with the One who allowed us to be their parents.

Neil Wilson

Our spiritual lives will be stretched by the challenges posed by our kids, as they question the reality of their youthful religious experience . . . and of ours. They may even seem to find pleasure in pointing out the hypocrisy in our church and in the way we live. And they may ask tough and profound questions about the Bible and theology.

Instead of fighting this, seize it as an opportunity to learn and grow. Walk with your child on his or her spiritual journey and grow deeper together.

WORDS FROM GOD ON MATURING IN FAITH

- "Don't let the excitement of youth cause you to forget your Creator. Honor him in your youth before you grow old and no longer enjoy living" (Ecclesiastes 12:1).
- "And I am sure that God, who began the good work within you, will continue his work until it is finally finished on that day when Christ Jesus comes back again" (Philippians 1:6).
- "Dearest friends, you were always so careful to follow my instructions when I was with you. And now that I am away you must be even more careful to put into action God's saving work in your lives, obeying God with deep reverence and fear. For God is working in you, giving you the desire to obey him and the power to do what pleases him" (Philippians 2:12–13).
- "You have been Christians a long time now, and you ought to be teaching others. Instead, you need someone to teach you again the basic things a beginner must learn about the Scriptures. You are like babies who drink only milk and cannot eat solid food. And a person who is living on milk isn't very far along in the Christian life and doesn't know much about doing what is right. Solid food is for those who are mature, who have trained themselves to recognize the difference between right and wrong and then do what is right" (Hebrews 5:12–14).
- "If you need wisdom—if you want to know what God wants you to do—ask him, and he will gladly tell you. He will not resent your asking. But when you ask him, be sure that you really expect him to answer, for a doubtful mind is as unsettled as a wave of the sea that is driven and tossed by the wind" (James 1:5–6).

OPEN HANDS

Another struggle for all parents, even Christian ones, is dealing with the twin illusions of control and ownership. We think we have our lives under control, and we try desperately to keep it that way. Then unexpected and unwanted events knock us back to the reality of our weaknesses and limits. Similarly, we operate under the assumption that everything we "possess" belongs to us, and no one dare mess with our possessions.

During a stewardship sermon or campaign, we temporarily adjust that thinking a bit as we respond to the challenge to "give back to God." But usually we continue to act as though our "tithes and offerings" are quite generous and that God should be pleased with what we give to him.

But here's the stark truth: *everything* belongs to God. It's all his—our cash, our investments, our homes, our necessities, our vehicles, our toys, our clothing and accessories, and (here's the kicker) *our children.* The Bible is quite clear that God owns everything and that he has entrusted it all to our care. As his stewards, we are to use wisely and invest wisely (see Matthew 25:14–30; Mark 8:34–36; Acts 4:32).

At our children's baptisms or dedications, we pledged, Hannah-like (see 1 Samuel 1), to give back our children to God. Knowing that God really owns our children and remembering that we pledged them to him should help us at this time of release. But still it's a struggle to truly let go. So hold your child with open hands.

Because your son or daughter is maturing, he or she will change in the spiritual area. When changes begin to occur, you can't do much except rely on God and encourage your student to be an honest seeker in his or her search for the truth. So during these days and months of spiritual change, keep the faith. Use it as a faith-stretching experience for yourself as well.

CONVERSATIONS

Adolescents are changing in every aspect of lives, even the spiritual area. And for many, the spiritual changes occur most dramatically after high school, as they discover their minds and learn to think critically. Watching and hearing our maturing children think through their faith and challenge ours can be painful. Yet it is an important part of the process of their understanding what they truly believe, owning it, and putting it into practice.

1. When did you profess your faith in Christ?

2. Thinking through your spiritual journey, in what ways did your faith change during the few years after high school? What caused those changes?

3. What differences do you see today in what you believe and in your relationship with God from five years ago? What were the catalysts, the causes?

4. In what areas might your son or daughter be an "environmental Christian"? How do you anticipate that changing?

5. What evidence do you have that your son or daughter is beginning to think through his or her faith and make it his or her own?

6. What challenges do you think your child will face in the next few years? Why?

7. What can you do to help your young adult mature spiritually?

Don't worry about avoiding temptation as you grow older. It will avoid you.
—Sir Winston Churchill

Chapter 11

RESPONDING WHEN THEY MESS UP

I don't know if you've noticed, but nobody's perfect. That includes us and our children. Daily we live out our finiteness and sinfulness. Sometimes our foibles result from limited knowledge or vision (for example, falling on ice, making a false assumption, misreading a label and then killing the flowers instead of the weeds, and so forth), and sometimes we simply make bad, self-centered choices (that is, we sin). Even perfectionists make mistakes.

So we shouldn't spend time wondering if our children will mess up—they will. That's life. Why should they be any different than we are?

I'm not suggesting that we send them off on their own with a fatalistic shrug and say something like, "If you can't be good, be careful." In fact, I think we ought to expect the best of our children and encourage them to make good choices and to do what is right and honoring to God.

And we need to pray for them and with them as they leave our homes and direct influence. A heart-to-heart talk will also help, assuming you haven't covered this area in depth already. Our kids need to know that we understand the prevalence and variety of temptations in their new surroundings.

During this talk, we should remind them of 1 Corinthians 10:13 where God says, "But remember that the temptations that come into your life are no different from what others experience. And God is faithful. He will keep the temptation from becoming so strong that you can't stand up against it. When you are tempted, he will show you a way out so that you will not give in to it." This passage points out that temptations are normal, that God is faithful and is with them during those temptations, and that God will give them a way out of the tempting situations. It also teaches that God will not allow our kids to experience a temptation that is too strong for them to handle.

So when temptation hits, they can pray, "Thank you God, for trusting me that much. Now what do you want me to do?"

They're called "helicopter parents" for their habit of hovering—hyper-involved—over their children's lives. Here at Colgate University, as elsewhere, they have become increasingly bold in recent years, telephoning administrators to complain about their children's housing assignments, roommates, and grades. . . .

"That's just part of how this generation has been raised," said Mark Thompson, head of Colgate's counseling services. . . .

For years, officials here responded to calls by biting their lips and making an effort to keep parents happy. But at freshman orientation here last week, parents heard a different message: Colgate is making educating students a higher priority than customer service. The liberal arts college of 2,750 students has concluded that helicopter parenting has gotten out of hand, undermining the out-of-the-classroom lessons on problem solving, seeking help and compromise that should be part of a college education.

Those lessons can't be learned if the response to every difficulty is a call to mom and dad for help.

Associated Press, "Colleges Try to Deal with 'Helicopter Parents,'" Chicago (IL) *Daily Herald*, sec. 1, August 29, 2005.

Then they can look for God's "way out" of the temptation and take it.

We don't expect our kids to be perfect; but we do expect them to live up to the high standards that they have already set for themselves before God.

CONSEQUENCES

So what happens when they fail to live up to those standards, when they mess up? If we truly want our children to grow up and become mature adults, we have to let them experience the consequences of their decisions. You probably have already been doing this for a couple of years, but here's where your resolve will be tested.

As loving and caring parents, we want to keep our children from experiencing any pain. Through the years, therefore, especially when they were younger, we usually rescued them and shielded them. We may even have acted as their advocates with certain teachers, coaches, and directors. Those days are over. We won't be nearby to swoop in for the rescue.

As we have become older and have experienced many struggles and strains, we have learned that life isn't fair and that sometimes the good guys get the shaft. So think how you will respond when the romance falters, the teacher is unjust, or the injury ends a season.

We have also learned that more often than not we cause our own troubles. So think how you will respond when your son or daughter experiences the natural and negative consequences of his or her poor choices.

Let's say, for example, that freshman Freddie calls home and reports that his grade point average has taken a tumble and fallen below the threshold for his scholarship. A rescue approach would have Dad giving him a stern lecture about studying more and then making up the difference in the tuition costs. It would be better if that father said something like this: "I'm sorry to hear that. Looking back, you probably wish you had studied more. How do you plan to make up the difference for that lost scholarship money this semester?" Freddie needs to experience the real and painful consequences of his actions (or, in this case, inaction).

A good rule of thumb is to never do for teenagers what they can do for themselves. There are exceptions to this rule, of course, but they are rare. Teens need to learn how to take care of themselves, to solve their own problems. When teenagers get themselves into trouble, we have two options. We can send in the lifeboats, or we can teach them to swim. The first option will save them this time, but the second will save them for a lifetime. Kids who experience natural consequences tend to become good swimmers.

Wayne Rice and David Veerman, *Understanding Your Teenager* (Lakeside, CA: UYT Books, 1999), 221.

Or suppose sophomore Suzie calls home and complains loud and long about her suitemates in the school apartment. At the end of the last school year, she had lobbied Mom and Dad for living there, with these girls, instead of the dorm, even though the cost was higher. A rescue approach would be for Suzie's mother or father to call the school and try to pressure the deans to fix the situation, to solve their daughter's problem. It would be better, however, to give this message to Suzie: "Wow—sounds like things didn't work out like you thought they would. What's your plan for resolving all that conflict?" Suzie needs to see that she got herself into this predicament and that she needs to make the best of it.

Other tempted-to-rescue situations could include becoming ineligible for a sport, going on probation for violating school rules, being charged by campus security or the police for various activities, running out of spending money, and so forth.

With increased freedom comes increased responsibility. And our emerging adults need to know what that means and live it. So unless the circumstances are, indeed, dire, don't rescue.

INTERVENTION AND RESCUE

At times, however, we must get involved. We will have to intervene.

In this regard, here's the basic principle to remember: get involved if the consequence will be too severe or if someone will be hurt badly. Consider these situations:

- Brent calls home and tells his sister, Brenna, that his college roommate is using drugs and has been on a scary high a few times. When Mom and Dad learn about this from Brenna (she was sworn to secrecy but let it slip one day), they call the school and talk with the dean of students.

The dean assures them that he will investigate without letting Brent know of their call.

This is a good example of when and how to intervene. Clearly someone could have been hurt badly (Brent and his roommate) by this destructive behavior. It's all right, and often preferable, to work behind the scenes in a situation like this.

- At break, Charlene's parents notice that she has lost considerable weight. When asked about it, Charlene answers that she has been working out a lot. After she returns to school, the parents talk to some of Charlene's friends and discover that these girls are alarmed as well. So they call the school counseling department and report that they think Charlene is suffering from anorexia nervosa.

Clearly the ultimate consequence of not eating is death—a bit severe. So someone had to get involved. Charlene's parents made the right decision.

Other intervention/rescue situations would include the following:

- References to possibly committing suicide (always take these seriously)

- Threats to a girl from an old boyfriend

- Evidence that a son or daughter may be sexually involved

- A pattern of anti-social behavior

- Talk that the student has been drinking a lot (for example, allusions by friends to his or her actions at parties or ball games)

- Symptoms of neurosis or worse

Most small schools, including all Christian colleges and universities, keep pretty good tabs on their students by way of resident assistants and others in the dorms, school counselors, faculty advisors, caring faculty, and small groups. (Note: this would be good to check out when considering educational institutions.) At larger universities, especially state schools, however, a student can be almost anonymous and lost if he or she wants to be.

On one of my visits to a high school campus (during my Campus Life ministry days), I asked a girl how her sister, Anne, was enjoying her freshman year at the state university. She responded that Anne had left and had gone across state to where her boyfriend was in school, at another state school, and was living with him. The sister knew about the situation, but not the parents. And if any of the resident assistants and dorm counselors of both institutions knew, which I doubt, they certainly didn't tell anyone. State schools are under great pressure to allow "privacy" and "lifestyle choice" and to treat these adolescents as though they were much older and more mature.

I don't mean to imply that state schools are evil and that our kids will be destroyed by matriculating there. But we need to be realistic—those institutions can be huge and very impersonal. So if your son or daughter is in that type of situation, look for creative but nonintrusive ways to get your information. But let's face it, you will have to trust him or her to do what's right. (We discussed this in chapter 3, remember?) If that trust is broken, then you'll have to act. But don't assume the worst.

If you believe that intervention is necessary, begin with a close friend to your son or daughter. Give a call and say that the conversation must be confidential. Then ask about the truth of what you have heard or seen—the bits of evidence, clues. Next, talk with a dean or school counselor and get his or her advice. Finally, you may have to confront your son or daughter directly. This will be most effective in person. You could go to the school and take your student out for a meal. Then you could lay out the evidence and express your concerns. At this point, you could also explain your expectations and the consequences for failure to meet them. The final step might be to remove the student from the university.

Sometimes intervention/rescue is the most loving act.

FORGIVENESS

In Jesus' parable of the prodigal son, recorded in Luke 15:11–32, the father released his younger son to take his inheritance early and set off on his own. The father didn't react angrily to his son's demand and kick him out of the house or abandon him, and he didn't mutter through clenched teeth, "Go ahead—mess up your life! But don't come running back here when you're broke and desperate!" Instead, the loving father allowed his son to leave and to live far away.

In the process, the son squandered his fortune. But all the while the father was waiting, scanning the horizon, ready to welcome his boy home.

Then, when finally the son returned, his dad didn't question his appearance or greet him with a typical "I told you so" speech. No, he did the opposite. As Jesus tells the story: "So [the son] returned home to his father. And while he was still a long distance away, his father saw him coming. Filled with love and compassion, he ran to his son, embraced him, and kissed him" (Luke 15:20)—and he threw a party! The father could offer a warm welcome and an enthusiastic embrace because no strings of offense and resentment were attached—just patient love.

That's the freedom release creates. Letting go lets you welcome back!

We know that the "father" in the story represents our heavenly Father. Thus his reaction parallels how God responds to us, to our poor choices and deliberate sins—our mess-ups. He waits for us to come to the end of ourselves (see Luke 15:17) and then come back to him. He loves us, has already forgiven us, and longs to have us back in fellowship, reveling in his love and forgiveness. It's so great to know and embrace that truth about God.

And it's the attitude we should model for our kids. They need to know that no matter what they do, we will always love them. That doesn't mean we will rescue them from every predicament and heal every self-inflicted wound; they will have to learn to deal with the consequences of their actions. But we're standing like the loving Father in Jesus' story, watching, waiting, and running—forgiving.

Will our kids mess up? No question about it. Will we forgive? I hope so.

CONVERSATIONS

As loving parents, we want nothing but the best for our children. And we certainly don't want to see them in pain. But sometimes experiencing painful consequences for personal choices and mistakes is the best way to learn from them.

1. What event from your childhood is burned in your memory as the time you learned that actions, poor choices, have consequences?

2. When have you tried to teach your child that lesson? What happened?

3. As you send this child off on his or her own, in what area are you most nervous about his or her messing up? Why?

4. Considering where your child will be, what steps will you take to intervene/rescue if you must?

5. When were you most aware of God's unconditional love and of his forgiveness? What evidence do your children have that you love them the same way?

Welcome back.
Your dreams were
your ticket out.
—Opening line of the
theme for *Welcome Back
Kotter* TV show
('75–'79)

Chapter 12

WELCOMING
THEM BACK
HOME

Whether your son has enlisted in the military and won't be home for at least a year or your daughter has enrolled in State U. in September and will be coming home for Thanksgiving, sooner or later your child will return. And he or she will have changed.

That's not bad, of course, but you will have to adjust.

ADAPTATIONS

Neil Wilson shares: "For Matt, the sudden transposition to a new world came as a shock. We didn't realize the depth of his experience until he came home for the first time and stood in the entryway weeping. Matt's personal character had stood up well to the usual rigors of basic training, but two remarkable transformations had come almost overnight. As if waiting to bloom under the surface, the faith that simply had been around him suddenly became intensely personal to our son. The pastor's-kid struggle that had made his own relationship with Christ hard to sort out came into startling clarity. Along with it came a new appreciation for what his home was worth."

Another parent explains that when her daughter went to Europe for a semester in college, she had to keep a journal of her experiences and feelings. After the daughter returned, she let her mom and dad read the journal. They were blown away by her insights and growing maturity. The mother reports, "We realized that our little girl had seen more and had absorbed more than we ever would have. Our daughter always had been independent, but she came home with more confidence."

Larry Kreider, who lived in Houston, Texas, at the time, took his son Brett to John Brown University in Siloam Springs, Arkansas, hundreds of miles away. About four weeks later, he and Susan attended the local high school homecoming game. He explains what happened: "A bunch of us from church decided that we were going to sit together at the game. At halftime, someone yelled out, 'There's Brett!' We were flabbergasted, excited, and had no idea why he was in town. Actually, Brett had been homesick and had decided to drive all night with a friend to be here for homecoming. As he walked closer, somebody else yelled out, 'He's got a ring in his ear!'

"So there we were. We hadn't seen our son in four weeks, we had sent him away to school, and he had an earring. Obviously we couldn't make a big deal out of it there. But later we asked him what it meant. The earring was nothing more than an expression of his identity—a very small 'rebellion' compared to other possibilities."

That was quite a shock, and a quick adjustment, for the Kreiders.

EXPECTATIONS

One of the biggest adjustments will be to your expectations. Often parents can hardly wait for the return of their son or daughter, looking forward to spending time together and catch-

When your kids return home, even for a short time, you are forced to make adjustments. Many of your normal routines are disrupted. Kids come and go at all hours. The house gets messy again. Most of the phone calls aren't for you. You feel guilty making him or her watch the news program that you always watch on Tuesday night.

When college students return home, it can be difficult. Even though you have the same house rules you have always had, things won't be the same. Your son or daughter will have had a taste of freedom and won't go back to being a child again.

Wayne Rice, *Cleared for Takeoff* (Lakeside, CA: Understanding Your Teenager, 2000), 215.

ing up. But then they hardly see the child because he or she has an entirely different agenda.

This can be a huge deal when a holiday such as Thanksgiving or Christmas with all the family traditions is involved. You may hear something like, "I don't want to go to Aunt Martha's; I have other plans!"

Sometimes parents can feel taken for granted, and they want to shout to their children-in-transition, "Hey, we've been paying for your life these past months. The least you can do is show some appreciation. What are we, chopped liver?" But the kid is off and running, with things to do, places to go, and people to see.

So it would be helpful to communicate ahead of time, to get it all out on the table. You should go over your expectations for the child when he or she is home. For example, who will decide on the schedule, what your child does and when? Be ready to compromise and to adjust your expectations, schedules, and rules, including curfew, visitors, meals, responsibilities, and interactions with the family.

I am not advocating total abdication of parental authority and responsibility. You will always be your child's parent, and he or she should honor and respect you as such. As the parent, you have the responsibility to care for your family and run your household. You wouldn't allow a houseguest to do anything he or she pleased. Why should you allow your son or daughter? Just remember, however, that your authority over your child is changing. And, if everything goes right, soon he or she will be totally on his or her own and completely out from under your authority and supervision.

And what about spring break? This can be another sore spot.

We had developed a family tradition of traveling to a warm destination for spring vacation. With Kara in college and Dana in high school, however, we discovered that they had different break schedules. And over the next few years, both girls, during their college years, had other ideas for spending that time, usually with college friends instead of family.

Again, we had to talk it out, negotiate, and come to a reasonable solution that would make sense for our family's needs (individually and collectively) and our budget.

The family dynamics will change; be ready.

CURFEW AND OTHER HOUSE RULES

As mentioned, another change relates to family rules and discipline. A college professor friend explained that he warns all his freshmen advisees about their first trip home: "Here, at the university, you can come and go as you please and set your own curfew. It's been nice—you have enjoyed your freedom. But when you go home, you will be directly under your parents' authority again and living by their rules. It will feel different, and you probably won't like it."

If you've been on a college campus lately, you've probably noticed that many of the social events begin after 10 p.m. About the time that you normally go to bed, they're just getting started. Have you tried calling a college student in the dorm? Many don't get to their rooms until midnight. When my nephew was a college junior a few years ago, he told me that his intramural basketball game was scheduled for ten thirty, and that was on a Tuesday night! Typical college students stay up late, sleep in when they can, and sometimes run for days on latent energy. Whether it's studying, playing sports or cards, ordering a pizza and talking with friends, going on a date, or just messing around, the late-night hours usually are used for everything except sleep.

Contrast this with the student's former life in high school. Because every day the class schedule was the same (for example: get up at 5:45 a.m., catch the bus at 7:10, go to classes all day, get out at 3:00 p.m., have practice, come home, eat dinner, study, go to bed), the regular routine demanded no late activities on school nights. On weekends, the schedule was relaxed, but still the curfew was eleven thirty.

Now put the high school and college schedules together—they don't match at all! And if you try to make them match, you'll have a problem.

Often it happens like this: Trent comes home from college for Christmas vacation, but he's rarely there. Instead, he's at Bob's or Jack's or shooting baskets at the Y or meeting friends at the show. Mom and Dad want to spend time with Trent, but they don't see him. They hear him come in at about 2 a.m., and they see him sleeping when they get up and out each morning (he sleeps till at least ten). But he's living like a college student, and they're living as they always have. Things have changed. This schedule is the opposite of yours at home. At about the time that you're winding down, they're winding up! If you're not prepared for this, you'll be in for a shock . . . and interpersonal conflict.

During Kara's freshman year at Wheaton College, she was home for fall break, essentially a long weekend in October. Because her college was only about forty-five minutes away from our house, a group of Kara's friends who hadn't gone home for the break decided to stop by to see her. They rang the doorbell at 10 p.m. and piled into our living room. We said they were free to hang out in the basement, and we asked that they keep it down so the rest of us could sleep. The evening was ending for us and just beginning for them!

Again, you should talk with your son or daughter and explain these differences without condescending or putting him or her down. Explain that you understand that he or she has grown beyond high school and hasn't been living under high school rules and regulations. Then discuss what a realistic curfew would be, considering the student's freedom and being considerate of the other family members. Also, discuss when the whole family could do activities together (for example, go out to dinner, go to a concert, sit in church together, and so forth). Come to a mutual understanding of the house rules and the penalties for disobeying them.

Another area of potential conflict is the use of the family car(s). If your student doesn't own a car or has left it behind, you may find yourself in serious negotiations over who is driving, when, and where.

Even if you have covered all of this in your pre-leaving talk, be ready for disagreements when your student returns, and be prepared to compromise.

SIBLING PRESSURE

If you have children still living at home, they will also be affected by the return of their brother or sister. So it would be a good idea to prepare them beforehand, explaining that their sibling is growing up and may act a little different. Also explain about possible adjustments to the family routines.

Young children may idolize an older brother or sister and anxiously await his or her return. Because I was in junior high when my youngest sibling, Phil, was born, I often would be called on to take care of him, serving as baby-sitter. So we spent lots of time together, and we bonded. About seven years later, I remember him standing in the stands and holding up a sign at one of my college football games. It read, "#72 IS MY BROTHER." We're still very close.

Children nearer in age, however, may have a different response, as we discussed earlier. They may resent the encroachment on what they now consider to be their turf. And some may react to all the attention lavished on the returnee (like the older brother's reaction in Jesus' parable of the prodigal son in Luke 15:25–30).

Regardless of your family's size or interpersonal dynamics, try to schedule some times together during the returning child's visit. Make them events of information (What has been happening in [the child's] life?) and celebration (Isn't it great that [the child] is back!). In addition to having certain meals together, you could do one of the following:

- Have a special evening out as a family, including dinner and a show.

- Throw a party.

- Rent a DVD and turn the family room into a theater, compete with popcorn and other snacks.

- Attend a big sporting event.

- Do something outside like having a picnic (in warmer weather) or going ice-skating (in colder climates).

The purpose of these events is to let all the children know that you're still a family, even though life is changing and the configuration of the family at home has changed.

So welcome your child home. You'll have to adjust, but it'll be great!

CONVERSATIONS

Through the years, you've watched your child grow, mature, and change. That process doesn't stop at high school graduation. In fact, some of the new physical, emotional, and intellectual changes can be dramatic. In addition, this child has enjoyed his or her freedom. So your son or daughter's return can cause complications on the home front.

1. What adjustments have you already experienced in your family dynamics?

2. What are your expectations for your child's involve-ment with the rest of the family when he or she returns?

3. What changes do you anticipate in your son or daugh-ter? What steps will you take to minimize the negative effects of those changes?

4. What potential conflicts with your child do you antici-pate concerning your house rules when he or she returns? What can you do to maintain the peace?

5. How do you think the other children will act during your son or daughter's stay? What can you do to make this a positive experience for everyone?

Don't be afraid of the time when your kids leave. It's really quite a nice season of life.
—Mary Manz Simon

Chapter 13

LOOKING DOWN THE ROAD

Consider these quotes about the future:

- "One faces the future with one's past."-Pearl S. Buck

- "The best thing about the future is that it only comes one day at a time."-Abraham Lincoln

- "I have but one lamp by which my feet are guided, and that is the lamp of experience. I know no way of judging of the future but by the past." -Edward Gibbon

- "In every conceivable manner, the family is link to our past, bridge to our future."-Alex Haley

- "Change is the law of life. And those who look only to the past or present are certain to miss the future."-John F. Kennedy

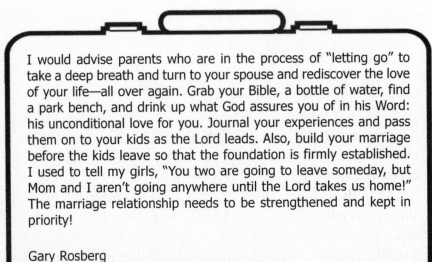

I would advise parents who are in the process of "letting go" to take a deep breath and turn to your spouse and rediscover the love of your life—all over again. Grab your Bible, a bottle of water, find a park bench, and drink up what God assures you of in his Word: his unconditional love for you. Journal your experiences and pass them on to your kids as the Lord leads. Also, build your marriage before the kids leave so that the foundation is firmly established. I used to tell my girls, "You two are going to leave someday, but Mom and I aren't going anywhere until the Lord takes us home!" The marriage relationship needs to be strengthened and kept in priority!

Gary Rosberg

- "These days people seek knowledge, not wisdom. Knowledge is of the past; wisdom is of the future." -Vernon Cooper

- "Look here, you people who say, 'Today or tomorrow we are going to a certain town and will stay there a year. We will do business there and make a profit.' How do you know what will happen tomorrow? For your life is like the morning fog—it's here a little while, then it's gone. What you ought to say is, 'If the Lord wants us to, we will live and do this or that.' Otherwise you will be boasting about your own plans, and all such boasting is evil."-James 4:13–16

Certainly we don't know much about what the future holds, but this much is clear: (a) we want to have one, and (b) we ought to be prepared for it.

Each of life's junctures and crises affords us the opportunity to think seriously about life—to learn from the past and prepare for the future. And nowhere is this more evident than at this time of letting go. So for a few moments, let's take a look down the road ahead.

YOUR MARRIAGE

The first bend in the road is your marriage because any stress on children puts stress on the parents, at the time of the significant event and in the days and years beyond.

Thus the drama of letting go can affect a marriage relationship, especially if one parent sides with the child against the other parent. This can happen on a variety of issues, beginning with the choice of college or university. Other potential areas of disagreement include spending money and jobs, extracurricular activities, travel plans, and other freedoms and responsibilities. This is more likely to occur in the present if the child has found it to be an effective strategy in the past. And it certainly is not a good idea for the future. Whatever the reason, allowing the child to pit one parent against the other is not good.

We have discussed several of the issues that are sure to arise, including new family dynamics, the child's growing pains, and adjustments during the return visits. For concerns and conflicts that arise at those times and others, good communication is imperative. So talk everything through with your spouse behind closed doors, and, if possible, come to an understanding. Then present a united front to your son or daughter.

Your marriage is more important than your relationship with your child. In fact, the best gift parents can give their children is a solid marriage. Having a mom and dad who love each other, are committed to each other, and work together in parenting builds a sense of security and safety in a child. Even though children often work hard at getting their way by trying to find a sympathetic ear with one parent, an ally, they really don't want parents to bicker, fight, and generally disrespect each other. And it hurts them in the long run. Future directions and decisions by and for your children will test your marriage. Keep your relationship strong.

THE EMPTY NEST

Another wide turn will occur when the last child leaves home and you face an "empty nest."

We have discussed, in depth, the feelings of loss at the release of a child and the adjustments when an older one leaves. So consider the shock to the system when we release the last one—when all the birds have flown away.

Teenagers' lives seem to be brimming with exciting activities. Phones ring, friends drop by, dates are planned and taken, permissions to use the car and extend the curfew are asked and then granted or denied, arguments rise and fall, TV and computer monitors glare, and music blasts. With limitless energy, adolescents seem to live in continuous motion and carry their parents with them. Even a home with just one teenager feels the effects.

The days leading to the child's exit also swirl with a whirlwind of activity, including shopping, packing, and good-byes to friends. Then Mom and Dad return home from the university . . . or the wedding . . . or the apartment . . . or the airport and are engulfed by silence.

I asked one mom what she and her husband missed most with all the kids gone. She answered, "I miss the laughter, the phone calls, and the excitement. I don't miss the 'Oh Mom!' stuff. But I miss the upbeatness of both the kids. Now it's very quiet."

Especially at first, the empty nest can be lonely. But there are other considerations.

Awkwardness

As mentioned earlier, many couples' lives have revolved totally around their children. Thus when the kids are gone, these parents are left with themselves. Larry Kreider explains: "At first you sit in the silence and think, 'What did we talk about before we had kids?' You also begin to realize why some couples get divorced after the children leave home; they hadn't spent time during those years filling each other's emotional tanks, and now they are empty."

Husbands and wives can feel awkward as they try to fill the silence and relate to each other again. Larry adds: "It's like starting over. You ask, 'Where can we go? What can we do?' It has all been put on hold for eighteen to twenty years.

Relief

Some couples feel relieved at this point, as though a great burden has been lifted from their backs. Maybe a son or daughter has found it difficult to become independent and leave home. Perhaps a grown child has returned for one reason or another. For these parents, having the home empty is a positive sign of progress in their kids' lives.

Chuck Lewis explains: "Sue and I felt considerable relief. Our youngest lived at home and went to a local junior college for a couple of years after graduation. Although Dan had more freedom, it was still a lot like when he was in high school. Sue, especially, had trouble resting until he came home at night. Quite naturally we were concerned about him.

"When Dan went off to New York to finish college, we felt freed from a sense of obligation and responsibility. And it gave

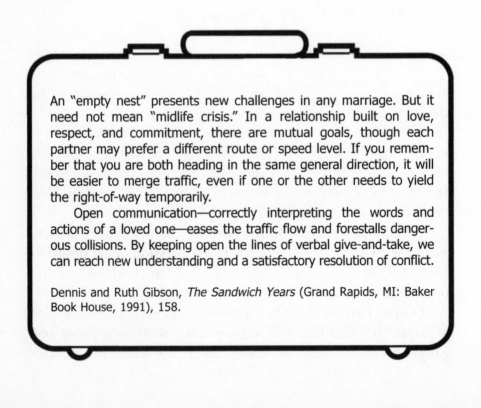

An "empty nest" presents new challenges in any marriage. But it need not mean "midlife crisis." In a relationship built on love, respect, and commitment, there are mutual goals, though each partner may prefer a different route or speed level. If you remember that you are both heading in the same general direction, it will be easier to merge traffic, even if one or the other needs to yield the right-of-way temporarily.

Open communication—correctly interpreting the words and actions of a loved one—eases the traffic flow and forestalls dangerous collisions. By keeping open the lines of verbal give-and-take, we can reach new understanding and a satisfactory resolution of conflict.

Dennis and Ruth Gibson, *The Sandwich Years* (Grand Rapids, MI: Baker Book House, 1991), 158.

us a lot of hope. Now we can recapture our time together without filtering it through our children's schedules."

We can be relieved to know that, for better or worse, our job as parents of growing children is nearly finished. Our children soon will be living and thriving on their own.

Adjustment

An important part of facing the empty nest involves adjusting to our changing roles with our nearly adult children. As we have discussed previously, the relationship is morphing from parent-to-child, where we, as parents, are always in control and meeting our children's needs, to peer-to-peer, where we and our children talk as adults and meet each other's needs. We are most deeply aware of this transition at the empty nest because all of the kids are in that stage or have gone through it.

Adjusting to having no children at home can be especially difficult for some women who have spent most of their adult lives being mothers. They have taken care of their sons and daughters and have gained much of their self-worth from their children. Backing off and becoming the child's friend can be difficult. One counselor-pastor puts it this way: "Usually, it is the mom who is in the nesting business. When her children are gone, it can be disastrous. She then may start to 'mother' her husband. I see this all the time in my ministry. And sometimes this need to mother pushes moms to ask their married daughters, 'Why don't you have children?'"

A husband reports, "Having both kids gone was a big adjustment for my wife—she still needed an expression of her desire to serve and meet needs. She found an outlet at church where she became very involved."

Dottye Luttrell describes another kind of adjustment. She explains, "It's hard for some women to see their once young and gangly daughters outshine them. Mom still wants that female dominance. But after you get through that, it's really nice having a comfortable friendship-relationship, where advice is looked for and appreciated, not resisted."

Men may also have difficulty seeing their sons pass them up—achieving more, earning more, leading more, gaining more notoriety, and so forth.

These adjustments can be awkward and even painful, but we must make them if we are to keep our marriages and families strong.

This dramatic change from having children at home to having none can be interpreted negatively as loneliness and loss. But it also can be very positive—a real benefit to having the kids gone. We can take advantage of this quiet to spend time in the Word and in prayer—"Be still, and know that I am God" (Psalm 46:10 NIV). We can read, think, journal, and plan. We can reduce the stress in our lives. So although it may take time to adjust to a home without children, we can discover and take advantage of the time, freedom, and quiet that this time of life provides.

We could spend another book discussing the empty nest. At this point, it's enough to know that down the road you will encounter new challenges and opportunities as you face life together, again, as just the two of you.

THEIR MARRIAGE

Speaking of the future, one of the most emotional experiences and toughest times of letting go is the child's wedding.

While discussing marriage in Matthew 19:5, Jesus quoted Genesis 2:24 and said, "This explains why a man leaves his father and mother and is joined to his wife, and the two are united into one." Did you catch that? The man must leave his father and mother.

One of the first public statements made in nearly every wedding ceremony is, "Who gives this woman to be married to this man?" The answer: "Her mother and I do." The father gives away the bride. That's truly "letting go."

During the high school years, we still feed, clothe, and house our children. During college, we pay the bills and give the kids a refuge and a place to come home. And some young adults continue to live at home or come back after they've been on their own for a while. In all these situations, regardless of the freedom we grant our sons and daughters, we still have a measure of control and close influence in their lives. But marriage is a public signal that they are moving out and on their own, establishing their own homes and families.

We're excited about the wedding and what it means for our young adults, but part of every parent dreads the day that they leave home forever.

Worries

Weddings elicit wide-eyed idealism, and this idealism causes us to mix worry with our hope. We know, from personal experience, that marriage takes work—hard work. Fortunately, if you have modeled a solid, committed, and loving relationship with your spouse, your children will have seen what a good marriage is supposed to look like, and they will likely repeat the pattern.

We also know, however, that marriages and families are under attack in our society these days. In fact, it has become increasingly difficult to stay married. More than half of all marriages end in divorce, and some studies report that the divorce statistics are similar for Christians. A few decades ago, divorce was almost a scandal, but these days it's easy to find someone who has been married three or four times. Living together has become socially acceptable, and promiscuity is viewed as the normal lifestyle for healthy singles.

Love American-style suggests that a person should find

someone to love, which, being interpreted, means someone who makes him or her feel good and who meets his or her needs, especially sexually. This message is promoted endlessly in popular culture. Because contemporary love is self-centered and feeling-oriented, young men and women make their pledges of undying love at the altar and then run from the marriages as soon as the feelings fade or personal needs change.

Many years ago (and in some cultures today), parents would arrange their children's marriages. The kids didn't first fall in love and then decide to marry; they had to learn to love whomever they married. Today, it is reversed; each person expects to marry the person whom he or she loves. Certainly we would not want to return to the days of arranged marriages. But we must realize that no matter what the dating-engagement-wedding routine, every married person still has to learn to love the person whom he or she has married.

These issues cause us to wonder how our children will fare . . . and we worry. And this can make letting go, giving away our child to another person, very difficult.

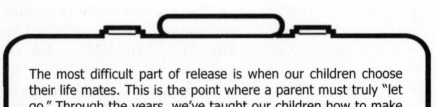

The most difficult part of release is when our children choose their life mates. This is the point where a parent must truly "let go." Through the years, we've taught our children how to make wise choices. We've modeled the decision-making process and prayed that God would lead them. But if I had it to do over, I would ask God every single day to send the right marriage partner for each of my children. I regret that I didn't pray often enough, hard enough. Don't make that mistake. Pray today and every day that God would lead your child to make the right choice.

Mary Manz Simon

Releasing Your Grip

Even when making a public commitment to a bride or groom, sometimes, the child does not want to leave home emotionally. The newlywed may have gone through the ceremony, but he or she still may be firmly grasping father's hand or mother's apron strings. That's when we parents have to exercise tough love, firmly but tenderly insisting that the son or daughter grows up, makes his or her own decisions, and becomes the husband or wife that God intends.

Often the opposite occurs; that is, the parents hinder a bride's or groom's leaving. Hating to see their baby grow up (or denying it), they continue to treat the adult child as though he or she were still in college or high school. I've heard of cases where the mother takes meals to the couple, does their laundry, and calls every day, in a pathetic attempt to keep her son or daughter close to home. In extreme cases such as that, the couple may have to move a few hours away in order to find space and make their own lives.

On this whole issue of letting go, I need to add a note for parents whose children are adults and still single. A wedding ceremony is a clear sign that this passage into adulthood has occurred for the child, but with older, single children, that passage is not so clear. Thus many parents continue to interfere in their older children's lives. We need to come to the point where we realize that they truly are grown up and on their own.

I'm sure you can think of other future occasions, other bends in the road ahead, where you'll have to release your single, adult child, again and again. It may be that you find yourself, unconsciously, grasping and pulling back, and then, realizing what you are doing, loosening your grip again.

AN UNFINISHED TASK

Years ago, at his seminars, Bill Gothard introduced and distributed a button that simply carried the letters PBPGNFWMY. That isn't a weird transliteration of a word in another language; it simply stands for an important concept and biblical truth, with each letter representing a word. The message? It's a request for the present and a statement about the future: "Please Be Patient; God's Not Finished With Me Yet."

We understand that the statement is true for our kids, especially when we watch them make immature decisions—when they act their age. They certainly are not finished products. At least we hope they will grow up.

But it's also true about us and about our relationship with our children.

About Us

We know that God works all things for our good if we love him and are fitting into his plans (Romans 8:28) and that his goal for us is to change us to be more like Christ (Romans 8:29). We also believe that he is working in us (Philippians 2:13) and that he will continue to do so (Philippians 1:6). And we understand that we won't be perfected until we get to heaven (1 John 3:2). So we shouldn't be surprised that God just might be teaching us lessons and changing us through this experience of letting go.

In the Book of James, God tells us, "Whenever trouble comes your way, let it be an opportunity for joy. For when your faith is tested, your endurance has a chance to grow. So let it grow, for when your endurance is fully developed, you will be strong in character and ready for anything" (James 1:2–4). While we probably shouldn't consider releasing our kids "trouble," the verse still applies, and the lesson is clear: when our faith is tested, we grow and become strong.

OF LEARNING AND LESSONS

- Deuteronomy 17:19-"[The king] must always keep this copy of the law with him and read it daily as long as he lives. That way he will learn to fear the LORD his God by obeying all the terms of this law."
- Deuteronomy 31:13-"Do this so that your children who have not known these laws will hear them and will learn to fear the LORD your God. Do this as long as you live in the land you are crossing the Jordan to occupy."
- Psalm 78:2-"I will speak to you in a parable. I will teach you hidden lessons from our past."
- 2 Chronicles 12:8-"But they will become his subjects, so that they can learn how much better it is to serve me than to serve earthly rulers."
- Psalm 119:7-"When I learn your righteous laws, I will thank you by living as I should!"
- Proverbs 4:5-"Learn to be wise, and develop good judgment. Don't forget or turn away from my words."
- Proverbs 12:1-"To learn, you must love discipline."
- Isaiah 1:17-"Learn to do good. Seek justice. Help the oppressed. Defend the orphan. Fight for the rights of widows."
- Isaiah 42:23-"Will not even one of you apply these lessons from the past and see the ruin that awaits you?"
- Jeremiah 35:13-"The LORD Almighty, the God of Israel, says: Go and say to the people in Judah and Jerusalem, 'Come and learn a lesson about how to obey me.'"
- Matthew 9:13-"Then he added, 'Now go and learn the meaning of this Scripture: "I want you to be merciful; I don't want your sacrifices." For I have come to call sinners, not those who think they are already good enough.'"
- Mark 8:17-"Jesus knew what they were thinking, so he said, 'Why are you so worried about having no food? Won't you ever learn or understand? Are your hearts too hard to take it in?'"
- Romans 5:3-"We can rejoice, too, when we run into problems and trials, for we know that they are good for us—they help us learn to endure."
- Philippians 3:17-"Dear brothers and sisters, pattern your lives after mine, and learn from those who follow our example."
- Colossians 3:10-"In its place you have clothed yourselves with a brand-new nature that is continually being renewed as you learn more and more about Christ, who created this new nature within you."
- Hebrews 5:12-"You have been Christians a long time now, and you ought to be teaching others. Instead, you need someone to teach you again the basic things a beginner must learn about the Scriptures. You are like babies who drink only milk and cannot eat solid food."

Earlier we discussed faith, noting how our children are changing and maturing in the spiritual area. But we should be growing spiritually as well. And this experience gives us an excellent opportunity. Here's how:

- Letting go should affect how we relate to moms and dads who are also going through this or who have experienced it in the past. At each stage of parenting, we gain empathy for others who have passed this way, especially our own parents. And we become better advisors and counselors.

- Letting go should strengthen our forgiveness muscle, as we forgive both our kids and ourselves for past commissions and omissions. Just as God has forgiven us, so we can forgive.

- Letting go should affect our dependence on God as we turn over to him what by far is most valuable to us. He has proven to be faithful in the past, and we can trust him for the future.

So be patient with yourself and the process. God isn't finished with you yet.

About Our Relationship

The task is unfinished in your relationship with your son or daughter as well. Think back to your dating years and then to your wedding. Regardless of how old you were when you got married, that ceremony and celebration marked the end of a long process. But it also marked the beginning of a new one: life together with your loved one—your new wife or husband. And just think how much you've changed and grown in that relationship through the years.

In the same way, releasing a child is the end of a long process. No wonder we sigh with relief. No wonder we feel so sad. But it also signals the beginning of a new era in your family and in your relationship with that son or daughter. You're not done living. You're not done relating. You're not done loving. You're not done growing. Certainly the relationship has moved to a different place—and we've discussed several of the growing pains—but you just may discover that the best is yet to come.

I also need to mention that although you have released this child, you always will be his or her parent. Yes, you should relate more like a fellow adult, a peer, a friend. But you'll have that something extra going for you in the relationship.

You'll have to be careful, of course, not to abuse your status as Mom or Dad. You know—manipulating through guilt, controlling actions through bribery, criticizing your child's lifestyle choices and parenting style, and, here's the biggie, saying "I told you so!" when your son or daughter learns life's lessons the hard way. Those are tempting actions to take but not very helpful.

And here's a thought: although you'll see yourself in your child (physical appearance, mannerisms, values, etc.), he or she is not just like you. That's okay too—one of you is enough!

CONVERSATIONS

No one knows the future, and we have no guarantees for a long and prosperous one. But as you look down the road, what can you imagine that you might face? And how do you think you'll react at each bump and bend?

1. In what ways has letting go of this child put stress on your marriage? What can you do to strengthen that relationship?

2. If this release empties the nest for you, how are you reacting? What will you do to make the empty nest experience positive?

3. Think back to your wedding day. How did your parents react? How did you know that they were truly letting you go?

4. Now imagine your child's wedding. How do you think you will react? What will make it a joyous occasion? How will you do at letting go?

5. Considering PBPGNFWMY, what evidence do you see of God's working in your life? What changes do you anticipate him making?

6. Project your relationship with your son or daughter in a couple of years. In what ways do you hope it will have changed and matured from what you have now?

APPENDIX

APPENDIX

BIBLE PASSAGES FOR THE JOURNEY
Verses That Every Graduate Should Know

- Deuteronomy 7:9-"Understand, therefore, that the LORD your God is indeed God. He is the faithful God who keeps his covenant for a thousand generations and constantly loves those who love him and obey his commands."

- Deuteronomy 31:6-"Be strong and courageous! Do not be afraid of them! The LORD your God will go ahead of you. He will neither fail you nor forsake you."

- Joshua 1:9-"I command you—be strong and courageous! Do not be afraid or discouraged. For the LORD your God is with you wherever you go."

- 2 Chronicles 7:14-"Then if my people who are called by my name will humble themselves and pray and seek my face and turn from their wicked ways, I will hear from heaven and will forgive their sins and heal their land."

- Psalm 9:9-10-"The LORD is a shelter for the oppressed, a refuge in times of trouble. Those who know your name trust in you, for you, O LORD, have never abandoned anyone who searches for you."

- Psalm 19:1-2-"The heavens tell of the glory of

God. The skies display his marvelous crafts-
manship. Day after day they continue to speak;
night after night they make him known."

- Psalm 23:1–6-"The LORD is my shepherd; I
have everything I need. He lets me rest in green
meadows; he leads me beside peaceful streams.
He renews my strength. He guides me along
right paths, bringing honor to his name. Even
when I walk through the dark valley of death, I
will not be afraid, for you are close beside me.
Your rod and your staff protect and comfort
me. You prepare a feast for me in the presence
of my enemies. You welcome me as a guest,
anointing my head with oil. My cup overflows
with blessings. Surely your goodness and
unfailing love will pursue me all the days of my
life, and I will live in the house of the LORD
forever."

- Psalm 46:1-"God is our refuge and strength,
always ready to help in times of trouble."

- Psalm 100:1–5-"Shout with joy to the LORD, O
earth! Worship the LORD with gladness. Come
before him, singing with joy. Acknowledge that
the LORD is God! He made us, and we are his.
We are his people, the sheep of his pasture.
Enter his gates with thanksgiving; go into his
courts with praise. Give thanks to him and bless
his name. For the LORD is good. His unfailing
love continues forever, and his faithfulness
continues to each generation."

- Psalm 121:5–8-"The LORD himself watches

over you! The LORD stands beside you as your protective shade. The sun will not hurt you by day, nor the moon at night. The LORD keeps you from all evil and preserves your life. The LORD keeps watch over you as you come and go, both now and forever."

- Psalm 139:13–14-"You made all the delicate, inner parts of my body and knit me together in my mother's womb. Thank you for making me so wonderfully complex! Your workmanship is marvelous—and how well I know it."

- Psalm 139:23–24-"Search me, O God, and know my heart; test me and know my thoughts. Point out anything in me that offends you, and lead me along the path of everlasting life."

- Proverbs 3:5–6-"Trust in the LORD with all your heart; do not depend on your own understanding. Seek his will in all you do, and he will direct your paths."

- Proverbs 13:20-"Whoever walks with the wise will become wise; whoever walks with fools will suffer harm."

- Proverbs 15:1-"A gentle answer turns away wrath, but harsh words stir up anger."

- Proverbs 16:28-"A troublemaker plants seeds of strife; gossip separates the best of friends."

- Proverbs 17:17-"A friend is always loyal, and a brother is born to help in time of need."

- Proverbs *18:24*-"There are 'friends' who destroy each other, but a real friend sticks closer than a brother."

- Ecclesiastes *12:1*-"Don't let the excitement of youth cause you to forget your Creator. Honor him in your youth before you grow old and no longer enjoy living."

- Isaiah 26:3-"You will keep in perfect peace all who trust in you, whose thoughts are fixed on you!"

- Isaiah 40:31-"But those who wait on the LORD will find new strength. They will fly high on wings like eagles. They will run and not grow weary. They will walk and not faint."

- Isaiah 53:5–6-"But he was wounded and crushed for our sins. He was beaten that we might have peace. He was whipped, and we were healed! All of us have strayed away like sheep. We have left God's paths to follow our own. Yet the LORD laid on him the guilt and sins of us all."

- Jeremiah *29:11*-"'For I know the plans I have for you,' says the LORD. 'They are plans for good and not for disaster, to give you a future and a hope.'"

- Lamentations 3:22–23-"The unfailing love of the LORD never ends! By his mercies we have been kept from complete destruction. Great is his faithfulness; his mercies begin afresh each day."

- Ezekiel 36:26-"And I will give you a new heart with new and right desires, and I will put a new spirit in you. I will take out your stony heart of sin and give you a new, obedient heart."

- Daniel 12:3-"Those who are wise will shine as bright as the sky, and those who turn many to righteousness will shine like stars forever."

- Hosea 6:3-"Oh, that we might know the LORD! Let us press on to know him! Then he will respond to us as surely as the arrival of dawn or the coming of rains in early spring."

- Zechariah 4:6-"Then he said to me, 'This is what the LORD says to Zerubbabel: It is not by force nor by strength, but by my Spirit, says the LORD Almighty.'"

- Matthew 5:15-"Don't hide your light under a basket! Instead, put it on a stand and let it shine for all."

- Matthew 6:31–34-"So don't worry about having enough food or drink or clothing. Why be like the pagans who are so deeply concerned about these things? Your heavenly Father already knows all your needs, and he will give you all you need from day to day if you live for him and make the Kingdom of God your primary concern. So don't worry about tomorrow, for tomorrow will bring its own worries. Today's trouble is enough for today."

- Matthew 7:12-"Do for others what you would

like them to do for you. This is a summary of all that is taught in the law and the prophets."

- Matthew 11:28–30-"Then Jesus said, 'Come to me, all of you who are weary and carry heavy burdens, and I will give you rest. Take my yoke upon you. Let me teach you, because I am humble and gentle, and you will find rest for your souls. For my yoke fits perfectly, and the burden I give you is light.'"

- Matthew 22:37–39-"Jesus replied, '"You must love the Lord your God with all your heart, all your soul, and all your mind." This is the first and greatest commandment. A second is equally important: "Love your neighbor as yourself."'"

- Matthew 28:18–20-"Jesus came and told his disciples, 'I have been given complete authority in heaven and on earth. Therefore, go and make disciples of all the nations, baptizing them in the name of the Father and the Son and the Holy Spirit. Teach these new disciples to obey all the commands I have given you. And be sure of this: I am with you always, even to the end of the age.'"

- Luke 11:9–10-"And so I tell you, keep on asking, and you will be given what you ask for. Keep on looking, and you will find. Keep on knocking, and the door will be opened. For everyone who asks, receives. Everyone who seeks, finds. And the door is opened to everyone who knocks."

- John 3:16-"For God so loved the world that he gave his only Son, so that everyone who believes in him will not perish but have eternal life."

- John 11:25-"Jesus told her, 'I am the resurrection and the life. Those who believe in me, even though they die like everyone else, will live again.'"

- John 14:6-"Jesus told him, 'I am the way, the truth, and the life. No one can come to the Father except through me.'"

- John 16:33-"I have told you all this so that you may have peace in me. Here on earth you will have many trials and sorrows. But take heart, because I have overcome the world."

- Acts 2:38-"Peter replied, "Each of you must turn from your sins and turn to God, and be baptized in the name of Jesus Christ for the forgiveness of your sins. Then you will receive the gift of the Holy Spirit.'"

- Romans 3:23-"For all have sinned; all fall short of God's glorious standard."

- Romans 5:1-2-"Therefore, since we have been made right in God's sight by faith, we have peace with God because of what Jesus Christ our Lord has done for us. Because of our faith, Christ has brought us into this place of highest privilege where we now stand, and we confidently and joyfully look forward to sharing God's glory."

- Romans 6:23-"For the wages of sin is death, but the free gift of God is eternal life through Christ Jesus our Lord."

- Romans 8:28-"And we know that God causes everything to work together for the good of those who love God and are called according to his purpose for them."

- Romans 8:38–39-"And I am convinced that nothing can ever separate us from his love. Death can't, and life can't. The angels can't, and the demons can't. Our fears for today, our worries about tomorrow, and even the powers of hell can't keep God's love away. Whether we are high above the sky or in the deepest ocean, nothing in all creation will ever be able to separate us from the love of God that is revealed in Christ Jesus our Lord."

- 1 Corinthians 10:13-"But remember that the temptations that come into your life are no different from what others experience. And God is faithful. He will keep the temptation from becoming so strong that you can't stand up against it. When you are tempted, he will show you a way out so that you will not give in to it."

- 2 Corinthians 5:17-"What this means is that those who become Christians become new persons. They are not the same anymore, for the old life is gone. A new life has begun!"

- 2 Corinthians 6:14-"Don't team up with those who are unbelievers. How can goodness be a partner with wickedness? How can light live with darkness?"

- 2 Corinthians 12:9–10-"Each time he said, 'My gracious favor is all you need. My power works best in your weakness.' So now I am glad to boast about my weaknesses, so that the power of Christ may work through me. Since I know it is all for Christ's good, I am quite content with my weaknesses and with insults, hardships, persecutions, and calamities. For when I am weak, then I am strong."

- Galatians 2:19–20-"For when I tried to keep the law, I realized I could never earn God's approval. So I died to the law so that I might live for God. I have been crucified with Christ. I myself no longer live, but Christ lives in me. So I live my life in this earthly body by trusting in the Son of God, who loved me and gave himself for me."

- Galatians 5:22–23-"But when the Holy Spirit controls our lives, he will produce this kind of fruit in us: love, joy, peace, patience, kindness, goodness, faithfulness, gentleness, and self-control. Here there is no conflict with the law."

- Ephesians 3:17–19-"And I pray that Christ will be more and more at home in your hearts as you trust in him. May your roots go down deep into the soil of God's marvelous love. And may you have the power to understand, as all God's people should, how wide, how long, how high, and how deep his love really is. May you experience the love of Christ, though it is so great you will never fully understand it. Then you will be filled with the fullness of life and power that comes from God."

- Philippians 1:6-"And I am sure that God, who began the good work within you, will continue his work until it is finally finished on that day when Christ Jesus comes back again."

- Philippians 2:12–13-"Dearest friends, you were always so careful to follow my instructions when I was with you. And now that I am away you must be even more careful to put into action God's saving work in your lives, obeying God with deep reverence and fear. For God is working in you, giving you the desire to obey him and the power to do what pleases him."

- Philippians 4:6–7-"Don't worry about anything; instead, pray about everything. Tell God what you need, and thank him for all he has done. If you do this, you will experience God's peace, which is far more wonderful than the human mind can understand. His peace will guard your hearts and minds as you live in Christ Jesus."

- Philippians 4:11–13-"Not that I was ever in need, for I have learned how to get along happily whether I have much or little. I know how to live on almost nothing or with everything. I have learned the secret of living in every situation, whether it is with a full stomach or empty, with plenty or little. For I can do everything with the help of Christ who gives me the strength I need."

- *1 Timothy 4:12-*"Don't let anyone think less of you because you are young. Be an example to all believers in what you teach, in the way you live, in your love, your faith, and your purity."

- *2 Timothy 2:15-*"Work hard so God can approve you. Be a good worker, one who does not need to be ashamed and who correctly explains the word of truth."

- *2 Timothy 3:16–17-*"All Scripture is inspired by God and is useful to teach us what is true and to make us realize what is wrong in our lives. It straightens us out and teaches us to do what is right. It is God's way of preparing us in every way, fully equipped for every good thing God wants us to do."

- *2 Timothy 4:18-*"Yes, and the Lord will deliver me from every evil attack and will bring me safely to his heavenly Kingdom. To God be the glory forever and ever. Amen."

- Titus *2:11–12-*"For the grace of God has been revealed, bringing salvation to all people. And we are instructed to turn from godless living and sinful pleasures. We should live in this evil world with self-control, right conduct, and devotion to God."

- Hebrews *4:15–16-*"This High Priest of ours understands our weaknesses, for he faced all of the same temptations we do, yet he did not sin. So let us come boldly to the throne of our gracious God. There we will receive his mercy, and we will find grace to help us when we need it."

- Hebrews 11:1-"What is faith? It is the confident assurance that what we hope for is going to happen. It is the evidence of things we cannot yet see."

- Hebrews 13:8-"Jesus Christ is the same yesterday, today, and forever."

- James 1:2–4-"Dear brothers and sisters, whenever trouble comes your way, let it be an opportunity for joy. For when your faith is tested, your endurance has a chance to grow. So let it grow, for when your endurance is fully developed, you will be strong in character and ready for anything."

- 1 Peter 1:3–4-"All honor to the God and Father of our Lord Jesus Christ, for it is by his boundless mercy that God has given us the privilege of being born again. Now we live with a wonderful expectation because Jesus Christ rose again from the dead. For God has reserved a priceless inheritance for his children. It is kept in heaven for you, pure and undefiled, beyond the reach of change and decay."

- 1 Peter 2:9–10-"But you are not like that, for you are a chosen people. You are a kingdom of priests, God's holy nation, his very own possession. This is so you can show others the goodness of God, for he called you out of the darkness into his wonderful light. 'Once you were not a people; now you are the people of God. Once you received none of God's mercy; now you have received his mercy.'"

- *1 John 1:9*-"But if we confess our sins to him, he is faithful and just to forgive us and to cleanse us from every wrong."

- *1 John 3:1–3*-"See how very much our heavenly Father loves us, for he allows us to be called his children, and we really are! But the people who belong to this world don't know God, so they don't understand that we are his children. Yes, dear friends, we are already God's children, and we can't even imagine what we will be like when Christ returns. But we do know that when he comes we will be like him, for we will see him as he really is. And all who believe this will keep themselves pure, just as Christ is pure."

- *1 John 4:10*-"This is real love. It is not that we loved God, but that he loved us and sent his Son as a sacrifice to take away our sins."

- *1 John 4:19*-"We love each other as a result of his loving us first."

- Revelation *21:4*-"He will remove all of their sorrows, and there will be no more death or sorrow or crying or pain. For the old world and its evils are gone forever."